BOLD FAITH RELOADED

DR. BRENDA JEFFERSON

Bold Faith Reloaded by Dr. Brenda Jefferson

BOLD FAITH: RELOADED

All Right Reserved.

Copyright 2024 by Dr. Brenda Jefferson

No part of this book may be reproduced or transmitted in any form or by any means electronic or mechanical - including photocopying, recording or by any information storage and retrieval systems- without permission in writing from the publisher except for quotes used in reviews. Please direct inquiries to:
scripturemusicgroup@livcc.org

Publisher: Scripture Music Group LLC
805 E Bloomingdale Avenue
Brandon, Florida 33511
brendajefferson.com

Your respect and support for this author is much appreciated.

NOTE: *All scripture cited in this book are from the King James Version / KJV of the Bible unless otherwise noted.*

ISBN: 978-1-7365465-7-4

ACKNOWLEDGMENTS

At a young age, God gave me the 'gift of faith.' It has been a divine source of strength and stability in my walk with Christ. As I reflect, I want to encourage you in your faith-journey. Let this book be a source of vigor and fortitude, as you continue to expand and go deeper in the Word of God.

Bishop M.B. Jefferson, I am so thankful for your steadfast love, and commitment to the call of God on your life. Thank you for all that you do for the ministry and our family. I thank God for you.

To My Children, each of you are unique and special, in gifting and purpose. As you lead with care, continue to keep God first and put the Word of God in your hearts, as you draw closer to Him.

To my Sons & Daughters in the Fellowship, each of you a part of W.A.F.I. (World Assemblies Fellowship International), Living in Victory Christian Church, & Deeper Life Christian Church; I take joy in seeing each of you prosper and helping you grow. This ministry is my delight. Let this book enlighten and encourage you as you make an impact for greater.

Bold Faith Reloaded by Dr. Brenda Jefferson

CONTENTS

1
LAYING THE FOUNDATION WITH BOLD FAITH

2
THE CALL TO HOLINESS
STEPPING INTO THE SACRED

3
BOLD FAITH UNDER FIRE
TRIALS AS A PATHWAY TO HOLINESS

4
LIVING BOLDLY IN HOLINESS

5
THE REWARD OF BOLD FAITH AND HOLINESS

Bold Faith Reloaded by Dr. Brenda Jefferson

BOLD FAITH RELOADED
AN INVITATION TO TRANSFORMATION

BRENDAJEFFERSON.COM

Welcome

to *Bold Faith Reloaded*. You are about to embark on a journey that transcends the familiar and ventures into the extraordinary. This book invites you onto a path of spiritual growth—one marked by courage, transformation, and deep fulfillment. Bold faith isn't just about taking grand leaps; it's about laying the essential foundation for a life of holiness—a life set apart, wholly dedicated to reflecting God's love and purity.

Faith as the Beginning

Faith is the starting point of our journey with God. It is the spark that ignites our relationship with Him. Through faith, our eyes are opened to His love, and our hearts learn to trust His promises. Yet, as powerful as faith is, it's only the beginning. To truly fulfill God's purpose for us, we must also pursue holiness—a journey that demands courage, persistence, and boldness.

In this book, you will see how bold faith serves as the foundation upon which holiness is built. By embracing both, you will be empowered to live the abundant, purpose-filled life that God has designed for you.

The Foundation and the Vision

Picture a bricklayer standing before an empty plot of land. In his mind, he envisions a grand mansion—a safe, beautiful place where his family can flourish. With great care, he begins his work, ensuring the foundation is strong and stable. But what if, after all that effort, he stopped? What if he never built the walls or added the roof? The dream of that mansion would remain incomplete.

Similarly, many of us start our journey of faith with enthusiasm, laying a solid foundation. However, we may find ourselves stuck, forgetting that God calls us not just to begin the journey but to keep building, growing, and stepping into the fullness of what He has prepared for us. The foundation of faith is essential, but it's only the start.

Bold Faith Reloaded encourages us to move beyond this initial foundation. It invites us to transition from the "milk"—the fundamental truths that sustain us as young believers—to the "meat"—the deeper truths that challenge, mature, and transform us. This is your invitation to take the next step: to build upon your faith foundation and pursue a life that is fully aligned with God's will, a life that is set apart in holiness.

The Call to Holiness

Holiness is not a burden or obligation; it is a divine invitation. God calls us to be set apart, to live in a way that reflects His love, purity, and power. This journey requires courage, commitment, and unwavering trust in God—and it all begins with bold faith.

Throughout this book, you will uncover how bold faith unlocks a life of holiness. You will learn how to take courageous steps, face challenges confidently, and live in a manner that reveals God's love to others. Remember, holiness isn't about achieving perfection; it's about persistence. It's about the willingness to grow, to be refined, and to become more like Christ every day.

The Key Message: From Faith to Fulfillment

Bold faith is the start of the journey, but it is in the pursuit of holiness that we align ourselves more deeply with God's will. Through holiness, we experience the fullness of His presence and the fulfillment of His purpose in our lives. As you read, our hope is that you will be inspired to embrace both bold faith and the call to holiness—that you will be encouraged to take the next step in your journey, to build upon your faith foundation, and to live fully in the purpose God has set for you.

This book is not just about acquiring knowledge; it is about transformation. It is about stepping beyond your comfort zone, accepting God's invitation to be set apart, and experiencing His incredible power and presence in every aspect of your life. If you are ready to say, "I want more. I am ready to grow deeper in Christ Jesus, to embrace the reality of heaven, and to boldly trust God no matter what comes my way," then join us. Together, we will explore *Bold Faith Reloaded* and step into the fullness of God's calling for our lives.

CHAPTER 1

LAYING THE FOUNDATION WITH BOLD FAITH

BRENDAJEFFERSON.COM

INTRODUCTION CHAPTER 1

THE FIRST STEP TOWARDS TRANSFORMATION

WHAT ARE YOU BUILDING YOUR LIFE ON FEAR OR FAITH?

In this chapter, we embark on the foundational journey of faith. Just like a builder starts with a strong foundation, our spiritual journey begins with bold faith. This chapter will explore how faith acts as the essential bedrock of our relationship with God and how we must continue building upon it to grow into a life of holiness. We'll look at how stepping beyond the basics of faith brings us closer to fulfilling God's purpose for our lives.

Section 1.1:

Faith as the Beginning of Spiritual Growth

Every great building project starts with a solid foundation. In our spiritual journey, faith serves as that foundation—it's the starting point upon which everything else is built. Without this strong base, anything we try to build will ultimately be unstable. In this chapter, we will explore how faith acts as the essential starting point and how we can lay a foundation that supports a life fully dedicated to God.

But remember, this is just the beginning. Our goal is to grow from this foundation of faith and experience true transformation and holiness. Let's delve deeper into what it means to build upon this foundation.

The Bricklayer's Vision

To understand faith's role in our spiritual growth, imagine the excitement of a builder dreaming of creating a beautiful mansion—a place where his family can thrive in safety and joy. The bricklayer begins his work with great care, knowing everything else will rest upon this base. He envisions laughter filling the rooms, warmth radiating from the walls, and the joy of family life flourishing within.

The foundation he lays is critical; without it, the walls would fall, and the dream would collapse. Similarly, faith is the foundation of our spiritual journey. It is the bedrock upon which everything else is built.

As believers, we need a foundation that is firm, stable, and capable of supporting the life God has envisioned for us. But we cannot stop there. Just as the bricklayer must continue building, we too must grow beyond the basics and press on toward spiritual maturity.

Angela's Bold Step of Faith

Consider Angela, who felt called by God to start her own business. Despite not having any prior experience and facing financial risks, she sensed in her heart that this was the direction God was leading her. With trembling courage, Angela took that bold step of faith. She laid the foundation by trusting in God's promises, equipping herself with the Belt of Truth, and reminding herself each day that God is her provider and guide.

Through prayer, persistence, and a willingness to trust, Angela's business began to grow. She faced challenges along the way—unexpected obstacles, sleepless nights, and moments of doubt. Yet, her foundation of faith enabled her to overcome every hurdle. Today, her thriving business stands as a testament to God's faithfulness. Angela's story shows us what it means to start a journey on the foundation of faith—trusting God with what seems impossible.

From Milk to Meat

Faith is only the beginning. As we grow, we must mature spiritually. In the Bible, spiritual growth is compared to moving from "milk" to "meat" (Hebrews 5:12-14). Milk symbolizes the foundational truths that nurture us as young believers. It is essential, but just as infants grow and require more than milk, we too must seek deeper truths to sustain our journey.

Bold Faith Reloaded challenges us to step into this next stage of growth. God calls us to a life of holiness, which requires more than the basics. It demands a deep commitment, a willingness to be transformed, and a dedication to building upon the foundation of faith.

Robert's Journey of Reconciliation

Robert's story is another example of moving from "milk" to "meat"—from staying safe to stepping out in boldness. Robert had been estranged from his family for years. Wounds ran deep, misunderstandings clouded any hope for peace, and reconciliation seemed impossible. Yet, God placed it on Robert's heart to reach out, to take a step toward healing.

Despite his fears, Robert chose to trust God with the outcome. He put on the Breastplate of Righteousness, allowing God's righteousness to replace his bitterness with grace. To his surprise, his family responded with open hearts, and together, they began the journey of reconciliation. Robert's faith became the foundation upon which the walls of healing and restoration were built. It was not just about reconnecting with his family—it was about demonstrating the transformative power of bold faith.

A Higher Calling

Building upon our foundation of faith is about stepping into a higher calling. Holiness requires us to move beyond comfort into growth. Faith is where we begin, but holiness is where God calls us to go. Throughout this book, we will explore how faith serves as the starting point, while holiness requires us to grow in God's truth and continually be transformed by His love.

Just as a bricklayer begins by laying a strong foundation, we too must establish a foundation of faith. This foundation is essential for everything else that will be built upon it. It is only the start of what God has planned for us. Let's look at more testimonies that illustrate how these courageous first steps in faith lead to deep spiritual growth.

Testimonies

- **Starting a Business on Faith**

    Angela, inspired by God to start her own business, felt uncertain and inexperienced. Yet, she chose to trust in God's promises and step out boldly. Angela armed herself with the Belt of Truth, grounding her confidence in the belief that God is her provider. Each day, she leaned into that truth, praying, working, and trusting God to guide her path. The challenges she faced—financial hurdles, setbacks, and doubts—became stepping stones that deepened her reliance on God. Today, Angela's thriving business is a testimony to the power of taking a bold leap of faith.

- **Reconciling with Family**

    Robert's heart ached with the weight of years spent estranged from his family. The journey to reconciliation seemed impossible—too painful, too complicated. Yet, God urged him to take the first step. Robert chose faith over fear, putting on the Breastplate of Righteousness, which allowed him to see his family not through the lens of past hurts but with God's eyes of grace. As he reached out, God began to restore what was broken. The result was more than just reconciliation; it was a testimony of God's healing power that only begins when we trust Him enough to act.

These stories remind us that spiritual growth begins with taking bold steps, even when we can't see the outcome. Laying a strong foundation of faith allows us to stand firm, grow, and move toward God's vision for our lives. This is only the beginning, but God's call extends beyond that. He invites us to continue building, growing, and embracing a life of holiness.

Key Verses:

Hebrews 11:1

Matthew 7:24-25

Faith is the foundation of our spiritual journey. It is the bedrock upon which everything else is built

THOUGHTS:

_____
_____
_____
_____
_____
_____
_____

BRENDAJEFFERSON.COM

Section 1.2:
Bold Faith in Action

Faith in Action Leads to Transformation

Laying the foundation of faith is an essential first step, but it's just the beginning. Faith must be put into action for it to grow and mature. In this section, we explore what it looks like to take that initial faith and put it into practice in our lives. Faith is not passive; it is active, dynamic, and transformational. When we step out in faith, we open ourselves to experiencing God's power in profound ways, and our lives are transformed.

Testimonies of Bold Faith in Action

To understand what faith in action truly looks like, let's look at Jessica's journey. Jessica felt God prompting her to serve in her church's outreach ministry. The thought terrified her—public speaking, praying with strangers, stepping into the unknown. She had always felt nervous about interacting with others, but deep within, she knew God was calling her to step out in bold faith.

Jessica decided to trust God to provide the courage she needed. She equipped herself with the Shield of Faith, which guarded her heart against feelings of inadequacy and insecurity. Nervously, she began to serve, and that was when she saw God work in ways she never imagined. She prayed for people in need, shared her story with others, and eventually started leading Bible studies. Her initial fear slowly faded as she saw God using her. Jessica's bold step not only transformed her life—giving her new confidence and purpose—but also changed the lives of those she served. Her story reminds us that faith becomes powerful when it is put into action. This is what it looks like to serve in ministry through bold faith.

Michael's Bold Step to Share the Gospel

Michael also struggled with the fear of sharing his faith. He worried about rejection—wondering if he would have the right words or if he might make a mistake. However, Michael sensed God calling him to share the Gospel and be a witness of His love. One day, as he noticed a coworker struggling with personal issues, Michael felt a strong nudge from God. This was his moment to act.

With shaky resolve, Michael put on the Shoes of the Gospel of Peace, trusting that God would guide him. Despite the doubt gnawing at the back of his mind, he began to speak to his coworker. To his surprise, his coworker was open, seeking comfort, and eager to hear more. They spoke at length, and Michael shared how God had been a source of hope in his own life. Eventually, his coworker accepted Christ. Michael's bold faith opened a door for someone else to experience God's love firsthand. This is what it looks like to overcome fear and share the Gospel.

The Necessity of Faith in Action

These stories illustrate that laying the foundation is just the beginning. For faith to grow, it must be put into action. It is not enough to simply believe—we must take steps that demonstrate our trust in God. Bold faith in action is what allows us to grow, experience God's power, and witness transformation in our lives and in the lives of others.

Let's explore more examples of individuals who put their bold faith into action and experienced God's transformative power.

Testimonies

- **Serving in Ministry**

  Jessica's story started with trembling hands and a heart filled with doubts, yet she was determined to obey God's call. She decided to step into the unknown, equipped with the Shield of Faith to guard her against feelings of inadequacy. Week after week, she faced her fears—stepping into unfamiliar situations, praying for people she did not know, and sharing her story. As she continued, Jessica's heart began to change. She saw lives being impacted—

people experiencing hope, healing, and comfort. Eventually, she even led Bible studies. What once seemed impossible turned into a beautiful expression of God's power working through her. Jessica's journey reminds us that God doesn't call the equipped; He equips those He calls. By putting her faith into action, she saw transformation not only in her life but in the lives of others.

- **Overcoming Fear to Share the Gospel**

  Michael's fear of sharing his faith had held him back for years. But when God prompted him to speak to his struggling coworker, Michael knew he had to act. It wasn't easy. As he approached his coworker, his mind filled with doubts—"What if I say the wrong thing? What if I push them away?"—but he chose to trust God. Michael put on the Shoes of the Gospel of Peace, determined to follow God's lead. He spoke with humility and compassion, sharing how Jesus had transformed his own life. His coworker, open and searching, found hope in Michael's words. That simple act of obedience led to his coworker eventually coming to know Christ. Michael's boldness in action was not only a victory over his own fears but also brought someone else into God's kingdom.

The Impact of Bold Faith

These testimonies show that bold faith must be put into action for transformation to occur. It is through acts of obedience—sometimes small, sometimes monumental—that we experience God's power in our lives. Bold faith is not passive; it requires movement, trust, and action. It invites us to step into the unknown with the assurance that God is with us every step of the way. When we do, we unlock the potential for God to work through us, witnessing His power in ways that exceed our expectations.

Key Verses:

James 2:17

Philippians 4:13

> Bold Faith Reloaded challenges us to step into this next stage of growth. God calls us to a life of holiness, which requires more than the basics

THOUGHTS:

_____
_____
_____
_____
_____
_____
_____

BRENDAJEFFERSON.COM

Chapter Summary

In this chapter, we explored how faith serves as the essential foundation of our spiritual journey. Faith marks the beginning of our walk with God—it is the anchor that roots us in His love and opens our hearts to His transforming power. However, faith is only the starting point. God calls us to build upon this foundation, growing into a life of holiness that reflects His love, purity, and purpose.

Through real-life testimonies, we witnessed the power of bold faith in action. We learned that it's not enough to simply believe; we must actively put our faith to work, taking steps that demonstrate our trust in God, even when the path ahead is uncertain. It is through these courageous steps that God's power is revealed in our lives, leading to personal transformation, the ability to overcome fear, and the strength to face challenges head-on.

When faith is active and alive, it allows us to grow spiritually and experience God's presence in new and powerful ways. As we build upon this foundation, we not only undergo transformation ourselves but also become instruments of change in the lives of those around us.

Reflection Points

1. **What is one area of your life where you need to lay a stronger foundation of faith?**
   Reflect on the parts of your life where fear, doubt, or uncertainty still hold you back. What steps can you take to strengthen your foundation of faith in those areas, trusting that God is in control?

2. **How can you move from "milk" to "meat" in your spiritual journey?**
   Spiritual growth requires moving beyond the basics and embracing deeper truths. Consider what steps you can take to deepen your relationship with God—whether it's through more focused Bible study, serving others, or committing extra time to prayer and reflection.

3. Reflect on a time when taking a step of bold faith led to growth or transformation in your life.
   Recall a moment when you chose to trust God despite the risks or uncertainties. How did God move in that situation? How did your faith grow as a result? How can you use that experience to encourage yourself and others in future steps of faith?

CHAPTER 1

FAITH REFLECTIONS
VERSES AND INSIGHTS FOR YOUR JOURNEY

HEBREWS 11:1

"Now faith is the substance of things hoped for, the evidence of things not seen."

WHAT IS YOUR FOUNDATION?

Reflect on whether you are building your life on the solid foundation of faith in Christ or relying on unstable things like fear or doubt.

FAITH AS THE START, NOT THE FINISH LINE

Consider how faith is just the beginning of your spiritual journey. What steps can you take to build on that foundation?

MATTHEW 7:24-25

"Therefore everyone who hears these words of mine and puts them into practice is like a wise man who built his house on the rock."

1 CORINTHIANS 3:11

"For no one can lay any foundation other than the one already laid, which is Jesus Christ."

TRUSTING IN WHAT YOU CANNOT SEE

Faith requires trusting in God's unseen promises. How can you exercise more trust in God's plan for your life, even when you can't see the outcome?

NOTES

CHAPTER 2

THE CALL TO HOLINESS
STEPPING INTO THE SACRED

INTRODUCTION CHAPTER 2

ANSWERING GOD'S INVITATION TO A HIGHER STANDARD

ARE YOU READY TO LIVE A LIFE SET APART FOR GOD'S PURPOSE?

Holiness is more than a set of rules—it is a divine invitation to live a life set apart for God. In this chapter, we'll explore what it means to step into a sacred, intentional life of holiness. Through real-life testimonies and biblical principles, we will see how choosing to walk in holiness deepens our intimacy with God and transforms every aspect of our lives. Discover how holiness empowers us to reflect God's character to the world.

....

....

....

....

....

....

Section 2.1:
Holiness as an Invitation

Holiness is not an obligation; it is an invitation—a divine call to step into the sacred and live in a way that reflects God's character. While some may perceive holiness as a set of rules to follow or a list of things to avoid, it is much deeper than that. Holiness is God's call for us to be set apart, to live in a way that mirrors His love, purity, and righteousness. It is an invitation to walk closely with Him, to embrace His way of living, and to experience the beauty of His transforming power.

Maria's Journey: Stepping into Holiness

To illustrate this concept, let's look at Maria's story. Maria faced a challenging situation at work—she was asked to participate in a business deal involving unethical practices. It would have been easy for her to go along with it, to stay silent and avoid conflict. But Maria knew that God had called her to a higher standard. She understood that choosing to honor God meant refusing to take part in the deal, even if it might cost her job.

Maria put on the Belt of Truth, anchoring herself in God's promises. She chose to trust that God would provide for her needs, even if standing for what was right meant facing consequences. As expected, her decision led to backlash from her colleagues, and she experienced moments of uncertainty, questioning if she had made the right choice. Yet, she remained steadfast, trusting in God's faithfulness.

Then, something remarkable happened. Maria's bold stand for holiness not only caught the attention of her superiors but also inspired some of her coworkers. They admired her courage and integrity. Eventually, a new and better opportunity opened up for Maria—one that allowed her to work in an environment aligned with her values. This is what stepping into holiness with bold faith looks like. It is choosing to honor God, even when it costs us, and trusting that He will honor our obedience.

Holiness as a Path to Intimacy with God

The call to holiness is fundamentally a call to intimacy with God. It is about drawing closer to Him, understanding His heart, and allowing His nature to transform us. We can think of ourselves as clay in the hands of the Master Potter. Just as a potter shapes and molds a vessel, God shapes us—He refines our character, molding us into vessels fit for His use.

To expand on this analogy, clay must be soft and pliable, yielding to the hands of the potter. In the same way, we must be willing to be transformed by God. We must allow Him to shape our hearts, smooth out our flaws, and mold us into vessels that reflect His glory. This transformation is not something we achieve on our own; it requires bold faith—a faith that trusts in God's ability to lead us, even when it requires us to leave behind our comfort zones and step into the unknown.

Equipping Ourselves with the Armor of God

To fully pursue holiness, we must equip ourselves with the Armor of God. This spiritual armor sets us apart and strengthens our ability to live in purity and dedication to God. For example, the Belt of Truth is vital for this journey. It anchors us in God's truth amid a world filled with lies and deception. Without the foundation of truth, we cannot effectively pursue holiness, as it forms the base upon which our transformation is built.

Additionally, the Breastplate of Righteousness plays a key role in protecting our hearts. It allows us to walk in integrity, reminding us that our righteousness is not our own but comes from Jesus Christ. It is His righteousness that empowers us to live in a way that honors God and enables us to move forward with confidence, even in the face of opposition.

Building Upon the Foundation of Faith

Just as we laid the foundation of bold faith in the previous chapter, we now build upon that foundation by pursuing a life that is set apart. Living a holy life means choosing God's way over our own, trusting in His plans, and believing that His ways are higher than the ways of the world. Holiness is not about perfection; it is about dedication. It involves continually turning to God, drawing closer to Him, and allowing Him to shape us into the people He has called us to be.

An Invitation to Stand Out

Holiness is an invitation to stand out. It is a call to rise above the noise of the world and embrace a higher standard—a standard rooted deeply in God's truth. It is an invitation to live with purpose, reflect God's glory, and be a light in the darkness. It means being willing to stand for what is right, even when it is unpopular, and trusting that God's way is always the best way.

Embracing Boldness in the Pursuit of Holiness

This journey requires boldness, as it often means standing against cultural norms and societal expectations. Holiness demands that we step into the sacred, confident that we are not alone. God is with us every step of the way. By equipping ourselves with the Armor of God, we gain the strength needed to withstand these pressures and remain steadfast in our commitment to holiness.

Maria's story is a reminder that pursuing holiness is not always easy—it often comes with challenges and sacrifices. But the reward is profound: a closer walk with God, a deeper sense of His presence, and the peace of knowing we are living in alignment with His will. As we embrace this invitation to holiness, we are stepping into the sacred—into a life that reflects the heart of God and draws others to Him.

Key Verses:

1 Peter 1:15-16

Romans 12:1

> Holiness is God's call for us to be set apart, to live in a way that mirrors His love, purity, and righteousness

THOUGHTS:

_____
_____
_____
_____
_____
_____
_____

BRENDAJEFFERSON.COM

Section 2.2:
The Narrow Path of Holiness

The journey of holiness is not easy; it is a narrow path that requires commitment, persistence, and ongoing spiritual growth. Jesus Himself spoke of the narrow path—the path that leads to life, but that few choose to take (Matthew 7:13-14). This is the path of holiness, and it is a journey that spans our entire existence. It calls us to continuously refine ourselves, lay aside the things that hinder us, and press on toward the goal that God has set before us.

James' Struggle for Freedom: Walking the Narrow Path

To illustrate what walking this narrow path looks like, consider James's story. For years, James struggled with a long-standing addiction that felt impossible to overcome. He knew that God was calling him to a higher standard—a life free from bondage and one of true freedom. There were moments when James felt overwhelmed and defeated, questioning if he would ever be able to overcome. But deep inside, he knew God was greater than his struggle, and he chose to trust God's power to bring him freedom.

James took the first bold step by seeking help. He joined a support group, immersed himself in God's Word, and surrounded himself with people who encouraged his journey toward holiness. He equipped himself with the Shield of Faith, trusting that God would give him the strength to resist temptation and persevere, even on the hardest days. There were moments of failure and times when he stumbled, feeling the weight of his struggle. But James refused to give up. Through God's grace and his commitment to holiness, he found the strength to get back up each time he fell. Slowly but surely, he began to experience breakthrough.

Today, James can confidently say that God has set him free. The addiction that once bound him no longer holds power over his life. Beyond freedom from addiction, James has discovered something even greater—a deeper, more intimate relationship with God. He knows what it means to walk the narrow path of holiness with bold faith, trusting God fully, and seeing His power at work in his life. James's journey is a powerful reminder that holiness is not about perfection; it is about persistence, trust, and surrender.

Continuing the Building Process: A Lifelong Journey

Building upon the foundation of faith is not a one-time event; it is a lifelong process. Just as the bricklayer does not stop after laying the foundation but continues to build, we too must continue to grow in holiness. This means continually seeking God, allowing Him to reveal the areas of our lives that need change, and surrendering those areas to Him. It also means allowing God to refine us, much like gold is refined in fire, so that we may reflect His glory more clearly.

Holiness is not a destination we arrive at; it is a journey we embark upon. It is about embracing the process, trusting that God is at work within us, and being willing to change and grow as He leads. Even when the path is difficult and the refining process feels uncomfortable, we can find comfort in knowing that God's ultimate purpose is to shape us into vessels that reflect His character and bring Him glory.

Equipping Ourselves for the Journey: The Shield of Faith

As we walk this narrow path, it is essential to equip ourselves with the Shield of Faith to withstand the challenges we encounter. The narrow path of holiness often requires deep trust in God, especially when we face trials and opposition. The Shield of Faith allows us to block the doubts, fears, and temptations that the enemy sends our way, keeping us steadfast in our pursuit of holiness.

Faith is our defense against the lies that tell us we cannot change, that we are too weak, or that our past mistakes define us. It is the shield that reminds us of God's power and faithfulness, giving us the courage to take the next step, even when the path ahead is uncertain. With the Shield of Faith in hand, we are able to move forward, trusting that God will provide the strength we need to keep going.

Guarding Our Minds: The Helmet of Salvation

In addition to the Shield of Faith, the Helmet of Salvation is crucial for guarding our minds. The mind is often the battleground where the enemy attacks, attempting to plant seeds of doubt, fear, and confusion. The Helmet of Salvation reminds us of our identity in Christ—we are saved, redeemed, and set apart for God's purpose. By renewing our minds daily and guarding our thoughts, we can live in holiness and align our actions with God's will.

The enemy seeks to fill our minds with lies—lies that tell us we are not good enough, that we are unworthy, or that God has abandoned us. But the Helmet of Salvation protects us from these attacks, enabling us to stand firm in the truth of who we are in Christ. We are children of God, deeply loved, and called to a life of purpose. When we remember this truth, we can walk in confidence, knowing that God is for us and that nothing can separate us from His love.

The Call to Transformation: Becoming More Like Christ

Holiness is about transformation. As Paul writes in Romans 12:2, it involves being transformed by the renewing of our minds. It is about allowing God to shape our character so that we become more like Christ. Holiness means being set apart for God's purposes and choosing to live in a way that honors Him in every aspect of our lives. Although this path is not always easy and requires sacrifice, perseverance, and a willingness to be different, it is the only path that leads to true fulfillment and joy.

When we choose to walk the narrow path of holiness, we are choosing a life of deep meaning and purpose. We choose to let go of the things that hold us back and embrace the life God has called us to live. We are choosing transformation—a transformation that begins with bold faith and is carried out by the power of God working within us.

Rising Above the Ordinary: Embracing the Sacred

God calls us to rise above the ordinary, to step into the sacred, and to live lives set apart for Him. This is the essence of holiness. It is a journey that requires us to trust God, grow in His truth, and be transformed by His love. As we continue to build upon the foundation of faith, we discover that the call to holiness is not a burden but a blessing—an invitation to experience the fullness of life that God has for us.

Holiness is not about following a set of rules; it is about living in relationship with God, drawing closer to Him, and allowing His presence to fill every area of our lives. It is about rising above the distractions of the world and focusing on what truly matters—our relationship with God and our calling to reflect His love and glory to those around us.

Embracing the Armor of God

Equipping ourselves with the Armor of God ensures that we are prepared for this journey, ready to face challenges, and able to walk boldly on the sacred path God has laid before us. By relying on His armor and strength, we can overcome every obstacle that might hinder us from living a life of holiness.

The path of holiness may not always be easy, but it is always worth it. As we equip ourselves with the Armor of God, we are reminded that we do not walk this path alone—God walks with us, empowering, protecting, and guiding us every step of the way. Let us embrace the call to holiness, trusting that God's grace is sufficient and that He will complete the work He has begun in us.

Key Verses:

Matthew 7:13-14

Romans 12:2

> Holiness isn't about perfection; it's about dedication. It involves continually turning to God, drawing closer to Him, and allowing Him to shape us

THOUGHTS:

_____
_____
_____
_____
_____
_____
_____

BRENDAJEFFERSON.COM

Chapter Summary

Holiness is not an obligation but a beautiful invitation from God to be set apart and live a life that reflects His love, purity, and righteousness. It is a journey that draws us closer to God, transforming us into reflections of His character. Throughout this chapter, we explored what it means to respond to this call—understanding that holiness is not merely about following rules but about embracing a deep, intimate relationship with God that reshapes every aspect of how we live.

We also learned about the importance of equipping ourselves with the spiritual armor that God provides to prepare us for the journey ahead. The Belt of Truth keeps us anchored in God's Word, the Shield of Faith guards us against doubts and fears, and the Helmet of Salvation reminds us of our true identity in Christ. Each piece of this armor is essential in helping us rise above the pressures of the world and embrace the higher calling that God has placed on our lives.

Holiness requires courage. It calls us to stand against cultural norms and embrace a life that is radically different—a life that shines the light of Christ to those around us. This journey may not always be easy, but it brings true fulfillment, joy, and a deeper intimacy with God. As we walk this narrow path, we can trust that

God is with us every step of the way, guiding, strengthening, and helping us to rise above the ordinary and step into the sacred.

Reflection Points

1. **What does holiness mean to you personally, and how can you actively pursue it in your daily life?**
   Take time to reflect on your understanding of holiness. What steps can you take each day to draw closer to God, to set yourself apart for His purposes, and to allow His love to shape your character?

2. **Which piece of the Armor of God do you need to put on to help you grow in holiness?**
   Consider the areas in your life where you face the most struggles. Which piece of God's armor—whether it's the Belt of Truth, the Shield of Faith, or the Helmet of Salvation—do you need to rely on more fully to help you stand firm in your pursuit of holiness?

3. **Are there areas in your life where you need the courage to be set apart and live according to God's standards?**
   Holiness often requires us to stand out and be different from the world. Ask God for the boldness to live according to His standards, even when it feels difficult.

CHAPTER 2

FAITH REFLECTIONS
VERSES AND INSIGHTS FOR YOUR JOURNEY

1 PETER 1:15-16

"But just as he who called you is holy, so be holy in all you do; for it is written: 'Be holy, because I am holy.'"

HOLINESS IS A CHOICE

How are you choosing to live a life set apart for God in your daily actions, decisions, and thoughts?

HOLINESS ISN'T ABOUT PERFECTION

Reflect on the idea that holiness is about dedication and growing closer to God daily, not about being perfect.

ROMANS 12:1

"Therefore, I urge you, brothers and sisters, in view of God's mercy, to offer your bodies as a living sacrifice, holy and pleasing to God—this is your true and proper worship."

EPHESIANS 4:24

"And to put on the new self, created to be like God in true righteousness and holiness."

GOD'S INVITATION TO INTIMACY

Holiness is an invitation to walk more closely with God. How can you draw nearer to Him by reflecting His love and purity?

NOTES

CHAPTER 3

BOLD FAITH UNDER FIRE TRIALS AS A PATHWAY TO HOLINESS

INTRODUCTION CHAPTER 3

TURNING YOUR TRIALS INTO TRIUMPHS

HOW CAN YOU TRUST GOD WHEN EVERYTHING AROUND YOU IS FALLING APART?

Faith shines brightest when tested by fire. This chapter dives into the refining nature of trials and challenges, showing how our faith grows stronger when we face adversity. We'll explore stories of individuals who have walked through fiery trials with bold faith, allowing God to mold them into vessels of holiness. Learn how facing hardship with unwavering trust in God transforms us and brings us closer to Him.

Section 3.1:
Faith in the Fire

In this chapter, we explore how bold faith is tested and refined during times of trial. Trials bring us face-to-face with our vulnerabilities and uncertainties, but they are also where God's power shines the brightest. Through real-life testimonies, we see how people's faith carried them through their most challenging moments, allowing God to shape them through every test. These stories are meant to inspire and encourage you, showing how God moves through our struggles and draws us closer to Him.

Testimony: Faith in the Midst of Financial Crisis

Consider Maria's story. She faced an unexpected financial crisis when she suddenly lost her job. The bills began to pile up, and Maria found herself in a place of uncertainty and fear. She could have easily given in to hopelessness, but instead, she made a choice—she chose to trust in God. Maria equipped herself with the Shield of Faith, refusing to let negative thoughts overwhelm her. She anchored herself in God's Word, holding onto His promise in Philippians 4:19: "And my God will meet all your needs according to the riches of his glory in Christ Jesus."

During this difficult time, Maria witnessed God's provision in miraculous ways. Friends and family came forward with support just when she needed it most, and eventually, she found a new job—one that turned out to be even better than her previous one. Maria's journey of bold faith under fire refined her character, deepened her trust in God, and allowed her to experience His faithfulness on a profound level. Her story reminds us that even in times of uncertainty, God is at work, using every situation to draw us closer to Him.

Testimony: Facing Health Challenges with Bold Faith

Another powerful example of faith in action is James' journey through a serious health crisis. When he received a diagnosis with little hope of recovery, fear threatened to overwhelm him. Yet, James chose not to let fear dictate his story. He put on the Helmet of Salvation to guard his mind against thoughts of hopelessness and despair. Day by day, he wielded the Sword of the Spirit, declaring God's Word over his life, including the promise found in Isaiah 53:5: "By His stripes, we are healed."

Despite the grim prognosis, James experienced a miraculous turnaround. His bold faith not only brought about physical healing but also drew him into a deeper relationship with God. James' journey became a powerful testimony to those around him—proof of God's ability to bring healing and transformation when we trust Him completely. His story shows us that even when the path ahead looks dark, God is our light, guiding us through every trial.

Faith Tested Under Fire

Every believer's journey includes moments of testing—times when our faith is put "under fire." It is during these trials that the true strength of our faith is revealed. While it is easy to have faith when everything is going well, it is the faith that stands firm during hardships that truly transforms us and draws us closer to God.

The story of Shadrach, Meshach, and Abednego provides a powerful example of bold faith in the face of extreme adversity. These young men were commanded to bow down to an idol, and their refusal to compromise their faith led them to be thrown into a blazing furnace. Despite the dire consequences, they chose to stand firm in their devotion to God (Daniel 3:16-18). Their faith was not dependent on a guarantee of deliverance but on the unwavering belief in God's goodness, regardless of the outcome. Whether God saved them or not, they trusted Him completely.

Their bold faith exemplifies the essence of trusting God even when the outcome is uncertain. They believed that God was with them, and their story shows us that true faith is not rooted in comfort—it is rooted in conviction.

Equipping Ourselves with the Armor of God

When we face trials, it is essential to equip ourselves with the Armor of God. The Shield of Faith is particularly important during these moments, just as Shadrach, Meshach, and Abednego used their faith as a shield against fear and doubt. We, too, must hold up our Shield of Faith to extinguish the fiery arrows of the enemy—doubts, fears, and temptations that arise in the midst of our trials.

The Belt of Truth also plays a crucial role during times of testing. The enemy often tries to deceive us when we are at our weakest, causing us to question God's goodness or our identity in Him. By grounding ourselves in the truth of God's Word, we can stand firm, knowing that God is faithful and that His promises remain true, no matter our circumstances.

Moving Forward

These testimonies and biblical examples teach us that trials are not meant to defeat us; they are meant to refine us. They are opportunities for us to put our faith into action, to trust God even in the most challenging circumstances. When we equip ourselves with the full Armor of God, we are prepared to face these challenges head-on, knowing that God walks with us through every fire.

Let us be encouraged by these examples. Bold faith under fire leads us to deeper intimacy with God, greater spiritual maturity, and a life that truly reflects His glory.

Key Verses:

Daniel 3:17-18

Isaiah 43:2

Trials are not meant to defeat us; they are meant to refine us

THOUGHTS:

BRENDAJEFFERSON.COM

Section 3.2:
Refined by Fire

As we continue our exploration of bold faith under fire, it is essential to understand how the refining process works in real life. Real-life testimonies provide a powerful glimpse into how God uses our trials to refine us, shaping us into vessels that reflect His glory. These stories show that the refining process is not just a theory but a profound reality for those willing to trust God through their most difficult moments.

Testimony: Overcoming Relationship Struggles

Consider Sarah's story. Sarah faced a difficult season in her marriage—constant misunderstandings, arguments, and moments when giving up seemed easier than holding on. The strain was overwhelming, and at times, she questioned whether her marriage could ever be healed. But deep down, Sarah knew that God could restore what was broken. She chose to believe that God's promises were greater than her circumstances. She put on the Belt of Truth, grounding herself in God's assurance for her marriage rather than believing the lie that it was beyond repair. She also equipped herself with the Shield of Faith, using it to guard her heart against bitterness and resentment.

Through persistent prayer, counseling, and a commitment to applying God's Word, Sarah and her husband began to experience healing in their relationship. God used that season of trial to refine Sarah's character, teaching her patience, forgiveness, and unconditional love. Today, their marriage stands as a testimony of God's redemptive power, showing how trials, though painful, can lead to transformation and holiness. Sarah's journey illustrates how bold faith amid trials can turn moments of brokenness into opportunities for growth and renewal.

Understanding the Process of Refining

The process of refining is not comfortable, and it is often painful. Just as gold is purified by being heated until impurities rise to the surface, our faith is refined through the challenges we face. The fire of trials reveals what is impure within us—our fears, insecurities, and the areas where we have yet to fully trust God. It is through these refining fires that God brings our weaknesses to the surface, allowing us to surrender them to Him and be transformed.

In James 1:2-4, we are encouraged to "consider it pure joy" when we face trials because these challenges produce perseverance, which leads us to maturity and completeness in our faith. This is the essence of the refining process—allowing the fire of trials to purify us so that we may grow in holiness and reflect Christ more clearly.

These moments of refining are opportunities to be set apart for God's purposes and to align our hearts more fully with His.

Equipping Ourselves with Spiritual Armor

During these refining moments, it is crucial that we equip ourselves with the Armor of God. One key piece of this armor is the Helmet of Salvation, which guards our minds. The enemy often tries to attack our thoughts during times of trial, filling our minds with doubts about God's love, fear of the future, and lies about our worth. The Helmet of Salvation reminds us of our identity in Christ—that we are saved, redeemed, and loved by God. It protects us from the enemy's lies, helping us stay focused on God's promises rather than being overwhelmed by fear and discouragement.

The Sword of the Spirit, which is the Word of God, is also vital when we are in the fire. It is our offensive weapon, allowing us to counter the enemy's lies with God's truth. Just as Jesus used Scripture to resist the devil's temptations in the wilderness, we too must wield the Word of God to combat the discouragement and fear that often accompany trials. The Word of God is powerful, and speaking it over our circumstances strengthens us, enabling us to endure and overcome.

Embracing the Fire as a Pathway to Holiness

The testimonies and biblical principles we have explored reveal that the trials we face are not meant to destroy us; they are meant to refine us. They are opportunities for our faith to grow, for our character to be shaped into the image of Christ, and for us to reflect God's glory more fully. Bold faith in the fire is what leads to true holiness. It is through these trials that God purifies us, teaches us to trust Him more, and helps us grow in ways we never imagined.

We must always remember that God does not leave us alone in the fire. Just as He stood with Shadrach, Meshach, and Abednego in the furnace, He is with us in every trial. The presence of God in the midst of our trials is our greatest assurance. Bold faith clings to this truth, even when the fire is at its hottest and the future is uncertain. As we walk through the fire, we find that the heat does not consume us; instead, it transforms us, drawing us closer to God and allowing us to experience His presence in profound ways.

Moving Forward

As we continue on our journey, let us choose to embrace the trials we face, knowing that they are opportunities for growth, deeper intimacy with God, and transformation. Let us equip ourselves with the full Armor of God, so that we may stand firm in the fire, be refined by it, and come out on the other side as vessels fit for God's glory. The refining fire is not something to fear; it is

It is during these trials that the true strength of our faith is revealed

THOUGHTS:

BRENDAJEFFERSON.COM

Bold Faith Reloaded by Dr. Brenda Jefferson

Chapter Summary

In this chapter, we explored how trials and challenges serve as a refining fire that helps us grow in faith and holiness. We learned that true bold faith is not only evident in times of ease but is proven in the face of adversity. Just like Shadrach, Meshach, and Abednego, who stood firm in the fiery furnace, we too are called to stand strong when our faith is tested. It is during these times of trial that God works most powerfully in our lives, transforming us from the inside out and deepening our relationship with Him.

Through the testimonies of individuals like Maria, James, and Sarah, we witnessed how God's presence in the midst of trials brings transformation. Maria found God's provision during a financial crisis, James experienced healing by standing on God's promises, and Sarah's marriage was restored through her unwavering commitment to trust in God's truth. These stories remind us that trials are not meant to break us but to shape us into vessels that reflect God's glory. When we face the fire with bold faith, we emerge stronger, more refined, and closer to God, ready to fulfill His purpose for our lives.

The refining fire is not something to fear but something to embrace, knowing that God is with us every step of the way, guiding, comforting, and strengthening us. Through each challenge, we have the opportunity to grow in holiness, become more like Christ, and experience His presence in a deeper, more intimate way.

Reflection Points

1. Think of a recent trial you have faced. How did your faith help you navigate through it?
   Reflect on a recent challenge in your life and consider how your faith provided strength or guidance. What aspects of your faith helped you persevere, and how did you see God at work during that time?

2. How can you use the Shield of Faith and the Sword of the Spirit when faced with trials?
   Think about how you can actively rely on the Shield of Faith to protect your heart from doubts and fears, and the Sword of the Spirit (God's Word) to speak truth over your circumstances. What steps can you take to equip yourself with these spiritual tools during times of testing?

3. What is one lesson you have learned from a difficult experience that has brought you closer to God?
   Consider a specific lesson you have gained from a past trial. How did that experience deepen your faith or draw you closer to God? How can this lesson continue to strengthen you in future challenges?

CHAPTER 3

FAITH REFLECTIONS
VERSES AND INSIGHTS FOR YOUR JOURNEY

JAMES 1:2-3

"Consider it pure joy, my brothers and sisters, whenever you face trials of many kinds, because you know that the testing of your faith produces perseverance."

FAITH GROWS IN THE FIRE

Consider how your faith is being strengthened and refined through your current trials. What might God be teaching you in this season?

GOD'S PRESENCE IN YOUR TRIALS

Reflect on the idea that holiness is about dedication and growing closer to God daily, not about being perfect.

ISAIAH 43:2

"When you pass throReflect on t assurance that God walks with yo through every hardship. How do knowing He is with you change yo perspective?ugh the waters, I will be you; and when you pass through t rivers, they will not sweep over yo

1 PETER 1:6-7

"In all this you greatly rejoice, though now for a little while you may have had to suffer grief in all kinds of trials. These have come so that the proven genuineness of your faith—of greater worth than gold—may result in praise, glory and honor when Jesus Christ is revealed."

PERSEVERANCE LEADS TO MATURITY

Challenges aren't meant to defeat you but to build endurance. How have trials in your life led you to deeper spiritual growth?

NOTES

CHAPTER 4

LIVING BOLDLY IN HOLINESS

INTRODUCTION CHAPTER 4

DAILY HABITS FOR A LIFE SET APART

HOW CAN YOU LIVE BOLDLY FOR GOD IN A WORLD THAT CONSTANTLY PUSHES AGAINST YOUR FAITH?

Holiness is not a destination, but a daily pursuit. In this chapter, we'll discover practical steps for living out holiness in everyday life. From renewing our minds to surrounding ourselves with a supportive community, we will learn how to cultivate habits that strengthen our spiritual walk. This chapter also highlights the boldness required to live set apart in a world that often opposes godly living, while showing the rewards of enduring with grace.

Section 4.1:
The Pursuit of Holiness in Everyday Life

Holiness as a Daily Practice

Living boldly in holiness is not a one-time decision but a lifelong pursuit. It involves a continual effort to align ourselves with God's standards and allow Him to transform every part of our lives. The call to holiness is both profound and practical—it involves the daily choices we make, the habits we cultivate, and the ways in which we seek God.

Imagine your heart as a garden. Each day, the gardener must water the plants, pull out weeds, and ensure they receive enough sunlight. If neglected, weeds will quickly overtake the garden, and the plants will wither. Similarly, we must be diligent in nurturing our relationship with God—removing the "weeds" of sin, feeding our spirits with the "water" of God's Word, and exposing ourselves to the "light" of His truth. Only through consistent, intentional care can we grow and flourish in holiness.

Holiness begins with renewing our minds. Romans 12:2 tells us not to conform to the patterns of this world but to be transformed by the renewing of our minds. This renewal is not passive; it's an active engagement, a daily decision to immerse ourselves in God's Word, maintain consistent prayer, and open our hearts to God's truth, allowing it to shape our thoughts, attitudes, and behaviors.

Practical Steps for Pursuing Holiness

The pursuit of holiness requires us to implement practical strategies every day. Here are some ways we can actively strive toward a life of holiness:

1. **Renewing Your Mind**

    The world constantly bombards us with messages that pull us away from holiness. It's easy to get caught up in society's values, prioritizing what it deems important over what God values. To pursue holiness, we must diligently renew our minds—aligning our thoughts with God's truth and rejecting the lies that try to sway us. Imagine each day as an opportunity to guard the garden of your heart, removing weeds of negativity, doubt, and temptation. Filling our hearts with God's Word is foundational to our growth and transformation.

2. **Anchoring Yourself in God's Word**

    Transitioning from renewing our minds, the next practical step is to anchor ourselves in God's Word. The foundation of bold faith and holiness is Scripture. Without a firm grasp of God's Word, it is impossible to grow in holiness. Picture it as building a house—Scripture is the sturdy framework that holds everything together. Daily reading of the Bible, spending time in prayer, and seeking to understand God's truth are essential practices. The more we immerse ourselves in God's Word, the more it shapes our character and helps us live in a way that honors Him. Without it, our lives could crumble under pressure, and the storms of life would threaten to tear us down.

3. **Surrounding Yourself with Like-Minded Believers**
Pursuing holiness is not a solitary endeavor; we need the support and encouragement of others. The early church thrived because believers were united in their pursuit of God—they encouraged one another, prayed for each other, and held each other accountable. Find a community of like-minded believers who can challenge, support, and walk alongside you. It's like climbing a mountain—having others makes the climb possible, and their encouragement keeps you moving forward, even when the path feels steep and overwhelming.

4. **Enduring Opposition with Grace**
While surrounding ourselves with fellow believers is crucial, we must also recognize that the pursuit of holiness often brings resistance. When we live differently from the

world, people may not understand; criticism or even persecution may follow. Bold faith does not shy away from the reality that living a holy life will invite challenges. However, holiness is not about fighting back; it is about enduring with grace. When the world questions your commitment, respond with love and patience, remembering that your life is a testimony of God's transforming power.

Testimony: Angela faced criticism at work when she chose not to participate in a dishonest practice. While others questioned her, Angela anchored herself in God's truth and responded with grace. Over time, her steadfastness led some of her colleagues to respect her integrity and inquire about her faith, illustrating how God uses moments of opposition to shine His light.

5. **Keeping Your Eyes on Jesus**

    To live boldly in holiness, we must keep our eyes fixed on Jesus. He is the ultimate example of bold faith and holiness. Jesus lived a life completely set apart—He walked in perfect obedience to the Father, even when it led to suffering. He is the author and finisher of our faith, and He has walked the path before us. By looking to Him, we find the strength and courage to live a life that honors God. Jesus is like a lighthouse for a ship at sea; when we keep our eyes on Him, we are guided safely through the storms and dangers of life.

Holiness as a Journey of Growth

Living boldly in holiness is not about achieving perfection—it is about pursuing growth. God knows we are imperfect, but He calls us to be continually transformed into the image of Christ. This transformation means letting go of old habits, changing our attitudes, and allowing God to refine us. It requires persistence in our pursuit of holiness, even when we fall short. God's grace is sufficient, and He is faithful to complete the work He has started in us.

Our journey of holiness can be likened to climbing a mountain. It requires effort, persistence, and sometimes a willingness to take a difficult path. There may be times when we slip or lose our footing, but we must keep climbing, trusting that God is our guide. Each step, no matter how small, brings us closer to the summit—the fullness of life in Christ. It's not about how quickly we reach the top but about continually moving forward, trusting that God will provide the strength we need.

This pursuit of holiness is a journey that requires consistency, courage, and community. As we remain committed to daily practices like renewing our minds, immersing ourselves in God's

Word, finding support from like-minded believers, enduring opposition with grace, and keeping our eyes on Jesus, we will grow and flourish in holiness. This is how we live boldly for God, setting ourselves apart as vessels for His glory and shining His light in a world that desperately needs hope.

Key Verses:

Romans 12:2

Psalm 119:105

Hebrews 4:12

Living boldly in holiness is not a one-time decision; it's a lifelong journey

THOUGHTS:

BRENDAJEFFERSON.COM

Section 4.2:

The Courage to Be Set Apart

Holiness Requires Boldness

Holiness is radical. It calls us to swim against the current of culture and embrace a life set apart for God. This kind of living demands courage—the courage to reject what is popular in favor of what is right, to hold fast to God's truth even when it means standing alone, and to live in a way that reflects God's standards rather than the world's.

To grasp why holiness requires boldness, we must recognize that pursuing holiness is not about blending in; it's about standing out. In a world that often values compromise, God calls us to rise above—to live according to His truth, no matter the cost. This journey takes bold faith. It means trusting that God's ways are higher and better, even when they stand in opposition to what society deems acceptable or desirable.

The Bible offers powerful examples of individuals who chose holiness over compromise. Daniel is one such example. Taken into captivity and living in a foreign land with different customs and beliefs, he refused to compromise his devotion to God, even when it put his life in danger. Daniel continued to pray, worship, and honor God, even when it meant being thrown into a den of lions. His story reminds us that holiness requires boldness—a willingness to be different, to be set apart, and to trust fully in God's provision and protection.

Testimony: Sarah's Stand for Integrity

Sarah, a young professional, faced a difficult choice when her colleagues pressured her to participate in a dishonest business practice. Though fearful of the consequences, she decided to stand firm in her values, knowing that God's truth was worth more than temporary acceptance. Her decision led to isolation at first, but over time, her courage and integrity drew respect from others and ultimately opened doors for her to share her faith. Like Daniel, Sarah's boldness became a beacon of light for those around her, illustrating the transformative power of living set apart.

The Cost of Holiness

As we move from understanding the boldness required to pursue holiness, we must also recognize that living boldly in holiness comes at a cost. It may mean losing relationships, being misunderstood, or even facing rejection. Jesus said that if we want to follow Him, we must be willing to take up our cross (Matthew 16:24). This means enduring hardship, making sacrifices, and placing God's will above our own desires.

Living a life of holiness is not for the faint of heart; it is for those willing to stand firm in their convictions, even when it costs them something. It is for those prepared to say no to the things of the world in order to say yes to God. This takes bold faith, a deep trust in God's goodness, and the belief that whatever we may lose for His sake will be more than worth it in the end.

Testimony: John's Transformation

Consider John, who lost friends when he chose to step away from his past lifestyle of partying and compromise. At first, he felt lonely and questioned if it was worth it. But as he immersed himself in God's presence, he discovered a peace and fulfillment that far surpassed the fleeting satisfaction he once sought. Over time, he formed new, life-giving relationships that aligned with his pursuit of holiness. John's story highlights that while holiness may come at a cost, the reward is far greater—a deeper intimacy with God and a life rooted in true purpose.

Standing Firm in the Face of Adversity

The cost of holiness is real, but it's important to also understand the rewards of standing firm. To live boldly in holiness, we must be prepared to face adversity. The world may mock us, question us, or even oppose us. Yet we are called to stand firm. Bold faith equips us to withstand the pressure to conform. It gives us the courage to hold fast to our beliefs, live according to God's standards, and trust that He is with us every step of the way.

Holiness is not about perfection; it's about persistence. It means being willing to get back up when we fall, continuing to strive for godliness, and trusting in God's grace to carry us through. The journey of holiness is about choosing, day by day, to live in a way that honors God, regardless of what the world may think or say.

Testimony: Leah's Stand for Faith

Leah faced intense scrutiny at her university for her beliefs. Her classmates often ridiculed her commitment to abstaining from certain behaviors that contradicted her faith. Leah felt the weight of rejection, but she chose to stand firm, knowing that her life was a testimony of God's love. Over time, she became a source of inspiration for others who were seeking truth, showing that standing firm in holiness, even when difficult, can lead to a profound impact.

Ultimately, living boldly in holiness is the highest calling we can have. It is a life fully surrendered to God, reflecting His character, and empowered by bold faith. As we pursue holiness, we begin to see that it is not a burden but a blessing—a way of living that brings true joy, peace, and fulfillment. It is a path that, while challenging, leads us into a deeper, more intimate relationship with God and allows us to live the abundant life He promises.

Key Verses:

Daniel 6:10

Matthew 16:24

2 Timothy 3:12

Holiness is not about perfection it's about persistence

THOUGHTS:

BRENDAJEFFERSON.COM

Section 4.3:

Equipped for Holiness – The Armor of God

The Armor of God as Essential Tools

To live boldly in holiness, we must not only pursue spiritual growth but also equip ourselves with the spiritual armor that God provides. In Ephesians 6:10-18, the Apostle Paul outlines the Armor of God—a set of spiritual tools designed to help us stand firm against the schemes of the enemy and maintain a holy life. Holiness is not only about setting ourselves apart; it is about being prepared for spiritual warfare. This armor ensures that we are protected, prepared, and ready to face the challenges that come with pursuing holiness.

Imagine a soldier gearing up for battle. Each piece of armor plays a critical role in defending against the enemy and ensuring readiness for the fight. Without these pieces, we become vulnerable to attacks that seek to weaken our faith and pull us away from God. As we explore each piece of the Armor of God, we will discover how it prepares us to live boldly in holiness.

> **Scripture Reference: Ephesians 6:11-17**
>
> *"Put on the whole armour of God, that ye may be able to stand against the wiles of the devil. For we wrestle not*

against flesh and blood, but against principalities, against powers, against the rulers of the darkness of this world, against spiritual wickedness in high places. Wherefore take unto you the whole armour of God, that ye may be able to withstand in the evil day, and having done all, to stand."

The Belt of Truth

The first piece of armor is the Belt of Truth. In a world filled with lies, deception, and confusion, truth is our anchor. Just as a soldier's belt secures their armor in place, God's truth holds everything together in our spiritual lives. To live in holiness, we must gird ourselves with God's truth. This truth serves as the foundation for every other piece of the armor, guiding our decisions, strengthening our integrity, and giving us the courage to live with honesty and transparency. Without truth, holiness is impossible, for we need a firm foundation upon which to build our character.

Testimony: Consider Tom, who was once caught up in a web of deception at work. The pressure to compromise his values seemed overwhelming, but he chose to cling to God's truth. Girded with the Belt of Truth, Tom refused to compromise, standing firm in integrity. Though it cost him popularity among colleagues, his bold stance eventually earned him their respect and opened opportunities to share his faith.

The Breastplate of Righteousness

Following the Belt of Truth, the next piece of armor is the Breastplate of Righteousness. Holiness is about living a life that is righteous before God. The Breastplate of Righteousness guards our hearts against the enemy's attacks—against doubt, shame, and condemnation that often arise when we strive to live for God. Just like a protective vest shields a soldier's vital organs, the breastplate protects our hearts. It reminds us that our righteousness is not our own but comes from Jesus Christ, shielding us from the enemy's accusations and lies.

> *Scripture Reference: Isaiah 59:17*
>
> *"For he put on righteousness as a breastplate, and an helmet of salvation upon his head…"*

This verse emphasizes the necessity of righteousness in our walk with God, protecting our hearts just as a breastplate protects a soldier in battle.

The Shoes of the Gospel of Peace

Beyond protection, we also need readiness, and the Shoes of the Gospel of Peace provide just that. These shoes symbolize our readiness to share the good news of Jesus. A soldier's shoes are essential for mobility, enabling them to march, move forward, and stand firm on uneven ground. In the same way, the Shoes of Peace equip us to stand firm and move forward in our calling. Living in holiness means not only being transformed ourselves but also becoming agents of transformation in the lives of others. These shoes help us walk boldly, carry the message of Christ wherever we go, and stand firm in our faith. As we pursue holiness, we bring peace and hope to a broken world, sharing the love and truth of God with those who need it.

The Shield of Faith

As we continue to understand the armor, we come to the Shield of Faith. Holiness requires bold faith, and the Shield of Faith protects us from the flaming arrows of the enemy—doubts, fears, and temptations. Just as a soldier's shield blocks arrows and attacks, the Shield of Faith deflects the lies of the enemy and helps us stand firm in the promises of God. Faith is what carries us through trials and challenges, enabling us to trust God even when circumstances seem impossible. Without faith, we cannot live in holiness, as it is the foundation upon which we build our trust in God.

Testimony: Rachel faced a season of financial instability that threatened to overwhelm her. Clinging to the Shield of Faith, she chose to trust in God's promises rather than succumbing to fear. In the end, God's provision not only met her needs but deepened her faith, reminding her that the shield is strong enough to withstand the fiercest of trials.

The Helmet of Salvation

Next, we need to protect our minds. The Helmet of Salvation guards our thoughts, shielding the mind—a battleground of spiritual warfare—where the enemy seeks to attack by sowing doubt, fear, and confusion. Just as a helmet protects a soldier's head, the Helmet of Salvation reminds us of our identity in Christ—we are saved, redeemed, and set apart for God's purpose. By renewing our minds daily and guarding our thoughts, we can live in holiness and align our actions with God's will.

The Sword of the Spirit

The final piece of the armor is the Sword of the Spirit, which is the Word of God. Unlike the other pieces, which are defensive, the sword is an offensive weapon. It allows us to take action, fight against the lies of the enemy, and stand firm in the truth. The Word of God is like a finely crafted sword that cuts through deception and darkness, bringing clarity and strength.

Scripture Reference: Hebrews 4:12

"For the word of God is quick, and powerful, and sharper than any twoedged sword…"

This vivid imagery shows that the Word of God is not passive; it is alive, sharp, and able to cut through deception, bringing clarity and strength.

Prayer as the Final Armor

Paul concludes his description of the armor with an exhortation to pray in the Spirit on all occasions. Prayer activates the armor, keeps us connected to God, and empowers us to live in holiness. It is through prayer that we seek God's guidance, find strength in times of weakness, and align our hearts with His will. Living boldly in holiness requires a life of continual prayer—seeking God's presence, His wisdom, and His strength.

Prayer is like the glue that holds all the pieces of armor together. Without it, even the strongest armor leaves us vulnerable. Through prayer, we maintain our connection to God, allowing Him to guide, empower, and sustain us as we face each day.

Living Boldly with the Full Armor

As we reflect on each piece of the armor, it becomes clear that living boldly in holiness requires the full Armor of God. This armor is not optional; it is essential. It equips us to stand firm against the enemy's attacks, live in righteousness, and be courageous in our walk with Christ. When we wear the full armor, we are empowered to pursue holiness without fear, overcome the challenges we face, and live a life fully set apart for God.

Living boldly in holiness is not just about our personal growth; it is about being a warrior for God, standing up for what is right, and being a light in the darkness. The Armor of God enables us to do this effectively. It protects, empowers, and ensures that we are ready for every battle as we pursue a life that reflects God's love and holiness.

Key Verses:

Ephesians 6:11-17

Hebrews 4:12

> Holiness is not a destination; it is a daily decision to choose God's way over the world's, reflecting His love in every thought, word, and action

THOUGHTS:

_____
_____
_____
_____
_____
_____

BRENDAJEFFERSON.COM

Chapter Summary

Living boldly in holiness is not a one-time decision; it's a lifelong journey that calls us to consistently align ourselves with God's standards and actively pursue spiritual growth. In this chapter, we explored practical steps for pursuing holiness daily, beginning with the renewal of our minds. Transforming our thoughts to align with God's truth rather than conforming to the patterns of this world is foundational. This renewal sets the stage for the choices we make and the actions we take, guiding us to live in a way that honors God.

We also discussed the importance of anchoring ourselves in God's Word. The Bible is our compass, guiding us through every challenge and helping us live a life of holiness. To grow spiritually, we must immerse ourselves in Scripture, allowing it to shape our hearts and direct our actions. Consistent prayer, meditation, and studying God's Word are essential practices in building a strong spiritual foundation.

Another key aspect of living in holiness is surrounding ourselves with like-minded believers who share our commitment to pursue God. We cannot walk this journey alone. The support, accountability, and encouragement we receive from fellow believers are invaluable, especially during difficult times. A community of believers becomes our strength as we strive to grow and mature spiritually, helping us remain committed and persevere through challenges.

Living boldly in holiness often requires us to endure opposition and criticism from the world. As followers of Christ, we may be called to stand against cultural norms, and this takes courage. Enduring opposition with grace means responding with love, patience, and unwavering commitment to God's truth. It is through our steadfastness that others witness God's love and power at work in our lives.

Throughout this chapter, we also learned the necessity of keeping our eyes fixed on Jesus, the author and finisher of our faith. He is our perfect example of how to live a holy and set-apart life. In Him, we find the strength, courage, and guidance needed to overcome obstacles and walk the narrow path of holiness. Holiness is not about achieving perfection; it's about being transformed daily by God's grace and continually moving forward in spiritual growth.

Lastly, we explored the significance of equipping ourselves with the full Armor of God—spiritual tools that help us stand firm against the enemy's schemes and walk boldly in holiness. Each piece of the armor plays a crucial role in defending our faith, renewing our minds, and empowering us to take action against forces that try to hinder our growth. Prayer is the key that holds the entire armor together, keeping us connected to God, empowered, and ready to face any battle.

Holiness is not about perfection—it's about persistence. It's about choosing God's way every day and allowing Him to refine and shape us as we draw closer to Him. It's about recognizing that we are set apart for a higher calling, living as a light in a dark world, and trusting in God's grace every step of the way. Through intentional daily practices, reliance on God's Word, and unwavering faith, we can live a life of holiness that glorifies God and draws us into a deeper, more intimate relationship with Him.

Reflection Points

1. **What daily practices can you adopt to help you pursue holiness?**

   Reflect on specific habits or routines you can incorporate into your daily life, such as prayer, Bible study, or meditation, that will help you draw closer to God and pursue holiness.

2. **How can you endure opposition with grace when living according to God's standards?**

   Consider how you can respond with love, patience, and humility when facing criticism or opposition for your beliefs. What practical steps can you take to remain steadfast in your faith?

3. **Who in your life can you lean on to encourage you in your journey toward holiness?**

   Think about the people in your life who share your faith and commitment to God. How can you build stronger connections with them for mutual support, accountability, and encouragement as you pursue holiness together?

CHAPTER 4

FAITH REFLECTIONS
VERSES AND INSIGHTS FOR YOUR JOURNEY

ROMANS 12:2

"Do not conform to the pattern of this world, but be transformed by the renewing of your mind."

LIVING SET APART

How can you live differently from the world, reflecting God's holiness in your actions and decisions today?

RENEWING YOUR MIND DAILY

Think about how your mind can be transformed by immersing yourself in God's Word and truth. What thoughts need to be aligned with God's perspective?

2 TIMOTHY 1:7

"For the Spirit God gave us does not make us timid, but gives us power, love and self-discipline."

HEBREWS 12:14

"Make every effort to live in peace with everyone and to be holy; without holiness no one will see the Lord."

COURAGE TO STAND FIRM

Living boldly in holiness requires standing firm in your faith. Where in your life do you need to be more courageous in living out God's calling?

NOTES

CHAPTER 5

THE REWARD OF BOLD FAITH AND HOLINESS

BRENDAJEFFERSON.COM

INTRODUCTION CHAPTER 5

LEAVING A LEGACY THAT REFLECTS GOD'S GLORY

WHAT LEGACY ARE YOU LEAVING BEHIND FOR FUTURE GENERATIONS?

Pursuing bold faith and holiness may come with challenges, but the rewards are eternal. In this final chapter, we'll reflect on the profound blessings that come from living a life fully dedicated to God—intimacy with Him, freedom from fear, and a life filled with purpose. We will also explore the legacy of faith and holiness we leave behind for future generations, multiplying the impact of our walk with God beyond our lifetime.

Section 5.1:
The Bold Reward

Intimacy with God and Inner Peace

Pursuing a life of holiness empowered by bold faith comes with challenges, but the rewards are immeasurable. One of the greatest blessings of living a life set apart for God is the deep intimacy we experience with Him. As we grow in holiness, we draw closer to God, gaining a deeper understanding of His heart and experiencing His presence in our daily lives. Bold faith invites us into moments where we must fully depend on Him, and in those moments, we find a connection with God that transcends anything the world can offer.

This intimacy brings with it an incredible peace—a peace that surpasses all understanding (Philippians 4:7). When we trust God with every aspect of our lives and walk in obedience to His will, we are liberated from the fears and anxieties that often overwhelm us. Holiness aligns us with God's purpose, allowing us to rest in His promises and find assurance in knowing He is in control. This peace is not temporary; it is a deep, abiding sense of calm that anchors us, no matter the storms we face.

Freedom from Sin and Fear

Another profound reward of pursuing holiness is the freedom it brings—freedom from the bondage of sin and the fears that once held us captive. Bold faith empowers us to confront the areas in our lives where sin has taken root. Holiness, then, becomes the process through which God sets us free from those chains. As we grow in holiness, we discover that the things which once enslaved us no longer hold power over us. We are no longer slaves to sin; instead, we are free to live the life God has called us to.

This freedom extends beyond sin; it touches our fears. With bold faith, we face our fears head-on, trusting that God is greater than any challenge we encounter. Walking in holiness gives us the assurance that God is with us, that He is our protector, and that nothing can separate us from His love. This assurance fills us with courage, enabling us to stand strong in the face of challenges, knowing that God is in control and will faithfully see us through.

A Life of Purpose and Fulfillment

Living a life of holiness also brings a profound sense of purpose and fulfillment. When we align our lives with God's will, we begin to understand the reason we were created. This understanding fills our hearts with joy as we serve God, love others, and become part of His greater plan for the world. Bold faith leads us into a life filled with purpose—a life that shifts our focus from personal desires to fulfilling the mission God has given us.

This sense of purpose is one of the most rewarding aspects of pursuing holiness. It gives our lives meaning, direction, and fulfillment. We are no longer wandering aimlessly; instead, we walk in step with God, confident that our lives carry eternal significance. The joy that comes from living a life of purpose is unparalleled—it is a deep, abiding joy that comes from knowing that we are exactly where God wants us to be, participating in His work and witnessing His power in our lives.

Key Verses for Meditation

Philippians 4:7

John 14:27

2 Corinthians 3:17

> The reward of bold faith and holiness is not just for us; it is for those who come after us

THOUGHTS:

_____
_____
_____
_____
_____
_____
_____

BRENDAJEFFERSON.COM

Section 5.2:
Leaving a Legacy of Holiness

A Legacy That Reflects God's Glory

Bold Faith Reloaded is not just about personal transformation; it's about creating a legacy that reflects God's glory. When we live boldly in faith and pursue holiness, our lives become a powerful testimony to God's grace and transforming power. We are called not only to be transformed ourselves but also to be agents of transformation in the lives of others. The legacy we leave is one of faith, hope, and love—a legacy that points others to God and inspires them to live for Him.

Holiness goes beyond our own spiritual growth; it's about impacting the world around us. As we grow in holiness, our lives begin to shine with the light of Christ, drawing others to that light. Our actions, our words, and our love for others become reflections of God's glory. This is the legacy we are called to leave—a legacy that brings others into the kingdom of God and inspires them to pursue a life of bold faith and holiness. When people see Christ's light shining through us, they are encouraged to seek the same transformation, multiplying the impact of our faith.

Multiplying Faith in Others

The reward of bold faith and holiness is not just for us; it is for those who come after us. When we live a life of faith, we inspire others to do the same. Our children, friends, and communities witness the way we live, and they are deeply impacted by our example. A life of holiness is a powerful testimony, capable of changing the lives of those around us and multiplying faith in others.

Consider the early church. The apostles lived lives of bold faith and holiness, and their example inspired countless others to follow Jesus. As a result, their legacy continues to this day, as the church has grown and spread throughout the world. In the same way, our lives can have an impact that reaches far beyond what we can see. When we live boldly for Christ, we leave a legacy of faith that will continue to inspire and transform others long after we are gone.

Eternal Impact

Ultimately, the greatest reward of bold faith and holiness is the eternal impact that our lives can have. When we choose to live for God, pursue holiness, and trust Him with every aspect of our lives, we invest in something eternal. The rewards of this world are temporary, but the rewards of living for God are eternal. We are laying up treasures in heaven, where they will never fade or be destroyed (Matthew 6:19-20).

The impact of a life lived in bold faith and holiness extends far beyond this world—it reaches into eternity. The lives we touch, the souls we lead to Christ, and the legacy of faith we leave behind—all carry eternal significance. When we stand before God, we will hear the words, "Well done, good and faithful servant" (Matthew 25:23), and we will witness the eternal impact of our lives. This is the ultimate reward—a life lived for God's glory, a life that has made a difference in the kingdom of God, and a life that will be celebrated for all eternity.

Key Verses:

Matthew 5:16

Hebrews 12:1

Proverbs 13:22

> When we live boldly for Christ, we leave a legacy of faith that will continue to inspire and transform others long after we are gone

THOUGHTS:

_____
_____
_____
_____
_____
_____
_____

BRENDAJEFFERSON.COM

Chapter Summary

In this chapter, we explored the incredible rewards of living a life of bold faith and holiness, including deep intimacy with God, inner peace, freedom from sin, and a profound sense of purpose. We also examined the powerful legacy that a life of holiness creates—one that impacts others, multiplies faith, and carries eternal significance beyond our own lifetime. Living boldly in holiness is not just for our personal benefit; it is a gift to future generations and ultimately brings glory to God.

This journey of holiness invites us to live in a way that not only transforms our own lives but also touches the lives of those around us, inspiring them to pursue God. As we grow in faith, we create a ripple effect that extends beyond our time, shaping the lives of others and building a legacy that honors God.

Reflection Points

1. How has your pursuit of holiness drawn you closer to God? Reflect on how your journey of faith and holiness has deepened your relationship with God. In what ways have you experienced His presence, guidance, and love more intimately?

2. What legacy of faith and love do you hope to leave for those who come after you?

    Consider the impact you want your life to have on others. What values, faith practices, or acts of love do you hope will inspire and guide the next generation?

3. How can the rewards of holiness motivate you to persevere, even when the journey becomes challenging?

    Think about the peace, freedom, and sense of purpose that holiness brings. How can these rewards encourage you to stay committed, especially during difficult moments, knowing that the ultimate reward is a life that glorifies God?

CHAPTER 5

FAITH REFLECTIONS
VERSES AND INSIGHTS FOR YOUR JOURNEY

MATTHEW 5:16

Let your light shine before others, that they may see your good deeds and glorify your Father in heaven."

LIVING FOR ETERNITY

How does focusing on eternal rewards change your perspective on the challenges and sacrifices you face today?

LEAVING A LEGACY OF FAITH

Reflect on how your faith and actions today will impact those around you and future generations. What legacy are you building?

PHILIPPIANS 4:7

"And the peace of God, which transcends all understanding, will guard your hearts and your minds in Christ Jesus."

MATTHEW 6:19-20

Do not store up for yourselves treasures on earth, where moths and vermin destroy, and where thieves break in and steal. But store up for yourselves treasures in heaven."

THE PEACE OF A HOLY LIFE

Holiness brings deep peace that the world cannot offer. How has living for God's purposes brought you peace in areas that once caused you anxiety?

NOTES

FINAL CHALLENGE
EMBRACE THE DIVINE CALL

BRENDAJEFFERSON.COM

Closing Thoughts

As we conclude this book, I want to leave you with a challenge: live boldly and fully embrace holiness. God has not called you to a shallow life but to the depths of His glory. This is not a simple calling; it is an invitation into a lifelong pursuit that is rich, profound, and transformative—a journey toward true fulfillment and eternal joy. It requires courage, persistence, and unwavering trust in God. It is a journey that begins with bold faith and leads to a life set apart for Him.

Perhaps, as you have read through these pages, you feel inspired but also a bit overwhelmed by the thought of what lies ahead. You might wonder if you can maintain this level of commitment or if you truly have what it takes to live a life of holiness in a world that often discourages it. I want you to know this: you do not walk this path alone. God walks with you, empowering each step you take, providing the strength you need, and placing people around you to encourage you along the way. His promise remains—He will never leave you nor forsake you.

If you are ready to say, "I want more. I am ready to grow deeper in Christ Jesus, to embrace the reality of heaven, and to boldly trust God no matter what comes my way," then take that step today. The journey will not always be easy, but it will always be worth it.

Embrace the divine call, pursue holiness, and live a life that reflects God's love and glory to the world. Let your life be a testament to the power of bold faith, a shining example of what it means to live fully for God. Let your every action, decision, and word be a reflection of His character, demonstrating to the world that God is alive and working through you.

Together, let us step into the fullness of God's calling for our lives and experience the incredible reward of bold faith and holiness—a reward not only for us but for generations to come, a reward that will echo into eternity.

The path to holiness is paved with moments of surrender, steps of courage, and consistent growth. It is the daily choice to rise above the ordinary and embrace the sacred. There will be days when you feel strong, inspired, and capable, and there will be days when you struggle, stumble, or even fall. But the beauty of this journey lies in persistence. The goal is not perfection—it is dedication, commitment, and reliance on God's grace every day. Holiness is not a destination; it is a continual journey of growing closer to God, becoming more like Him, and living in His truth.

As you reflect on all you have read and begin to consider the next steps, remember that each day is an opportunity for a fresh start. God's mercies are new every morning. Each day, you have the chance to rise, walk boldly in faith, and embrace the call to holiness with a renewed heart.

A New Beginning: 30 Days to Bold Faith

The end of this book is not truly the end, but the beginning of something deeper and more profound. As you complete these pages, I want to invite you to continue this journey of transformation intentionally. The next 30 days are an opportunity to put all that you've learned into practice—a journey designed to cultivate bold faith, grow in holiness, and experience God's presence in every aspect of your life.

This 30-Day Journey to Bold Faith is more than a challenge; it is a commitment to prioritize your spiritual growth. Each day offers a chance to build upon the foundation of faith you've laid, strengthen your spirit, and walk more closely with God. You will find practical actions, reflections, and scriptures that will not only inspire you but also help you live out the truth you have embraced.

Every day is a step. Some days will be steps of reflection, while others will be steps of action. There will be days of breakthroughs and days of quiet but steady growth. Each moment you invest will bring you closer to the person God has called you to be—someone living fully in bold faith and radiant holiness.

This journey is designed to be a tangible way to cultivate the habits and mindset that foster a life of holiness. As you embark on this 30-day journey, you will not be alone. I encourage you to reach out to friends or family members who might join you, creating a community of accountability and shared growth. Let this be a time of transformation that doesn't end after thirty days but ignites a lifetime of deeper faith and commitment to God.

If you are ready, take the next step and begin this journey. Let these 30 days be a catalyst for growth that extends into a lifetime. Let this be the season where your bold faith truly comes alive, where your commitment to holiness takes root, and where you experience God's love in ways you never imagined. As you commit to these next 30 days, I believe you will see God move in miraculous ways, transforming your heart, renewing your mind, and equipping you for the life He has called you to live.

The reward of bold faith and holiness is intimacy with God, inner peace, a life of purpose, and a legacy that extends into eternity. Embrace this moment, this opportunity, and this divine call. Step boldly into the future, knowing that God is with you every step of the way, guiding you, empowering you, and drawing you ever closer to Him.

Let's Begin the Journey Together

As we close this book, my prayer is that you are filled with hope and excitement for what lies ahead. You have been called to a life that is extraordinary—a life filled with purpose, power, and presence. Embrace that call. Take the next step with courage and boldness, knowing that God is leading you on a journey of transformation and growth.

Remember, you are not alone. God is with you, and this community of faith is cheering you on. Let's take this journey together and witness the amazing things God will do in and through our lives as we live boldly in faith and holiness. Your next chapter starts now—let's write it together.

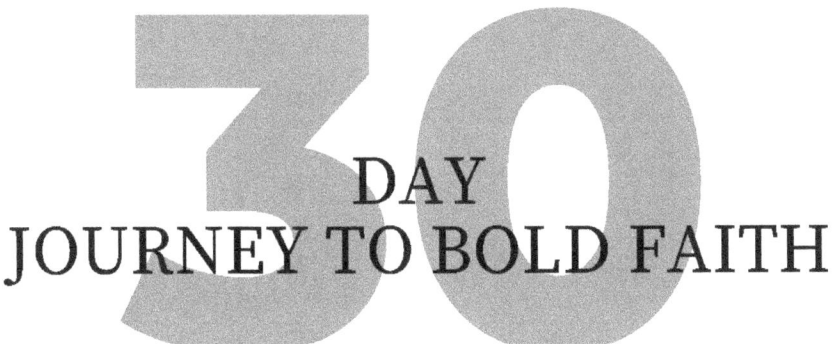

DAY
JOURNEY TO BOLD FAITH

A NEW BEGINNING
TO TRANSFORMATIVE FAITH

This journal belongs to:

_____

_____

BRENDAJEFFERSON.COM

INTRODUCTION JOURNAL

30-DAY JOURNEY TO BOLD FAITH
A NEW BEGINNING TO TRANSFORMATIVE FAITH

ARE YOU READY TO EXPERIENCE A DEEPER LEVEL OF FAITH AND DISCOVER GOD'S PURPOSE FOR YOUR LIFE IN A POWERFUL WAY?

This 30-Day Journey is not just a daily checklist or routine—it is an invitation to step into a transformative experience where your faith is strengthened, your heart is opened, and your spirit is refreshed. Over the next four weeks, you will explore practical ways to live boldly in faith, drawing closer to God and discovering the abundant life He has in store for you.

Each day has been carefully designed to guide you through scripture, reflection, and action, creating moments of real spiritual growth. Whether you're laying th foundation of faith, learning to trust God more deeply, or building confidence ir His promises, this journey is about transformation—from the inside out.

This isn't just a workbook; it's a pathway to a renewed relationship with God, a time to let His Word shape your thoughts, decisions, and future. As you progress through these daily exercises, you'll begin to see how your faith is building and how God is working in every area of your life.

You'll face challenges that call you to trust, take bold steps of action, and experience God's presence in ways you may have never imagined. Along this journey, you'll uncover what it truly means to live a life of bold faith, from trusting God in the unseen to walking in His purpose daily.

So, are you ready to take the first step? Let's embark on this life-changing journe together, committing to 30 days of pursuing God with boldness and expectation. Get ready to transform your faith and step into the fullness of God's plan for you

Let the journey begin.

30 DAY JOURNEY TO BOLD FAITH

Week 1 " Laying the Foundation of Bold Faith"   Date ____ / ____ / ____

Day 1: Understand Faith

How do you feel today?

Choose a face

Add a description _____

_____

_____

READ:

Hebrews 11:1

"Now faith is the substance of things hoped for, the evidence of things not seen."

REFLECT:

What does faith mean to you personally?

_____

_____

_____

_____

_____

_____

ACTION:

Write down your understanding of faith. This verse helps you realize that faith is about believing in what you cannot see. By articulating your own understanding, you begin to internalize what faith means and set the stage for a deeper, more personal connection with God.

_____

_____

_____

_____

_____

BRENDAJEFFERSON.COM

30 DAY JOURNEY TO BOLD FAITH

Week 1 " Laying the Foundation of Bold Faith" Date ___ / ___ / ___

Day 2: Seek God

How do you feel today?

Choose a face 😃 😊 😐 🙁 😣 😠

Add a description _____

_____

_____

READ:

Matthew 6:33

"But seek first the kingdom of God and His righteousness, and all these things shall be added to you."

REFLECT:

Think about what it means to seek God first in your life. How can you put God at the forefront of your life?

ACTION:

Make a list of ways you can prioritize God daily. This verse emphasizes putting God first. By listing practical ways to seek Him, such as starting your day with prayer or reading scripture, you actively place God at the center of your life.

BRENDAJEFFERSON.COM

30 DAY JOURNEY TO BOLD FAITH

Week 1 "Laying the Foundation of Bold Faith"   Date ____ / ____ / ____

Day 3: Trust in God

How do you feel today?

Choose a face   😃 🙂 😐 🙁 😣 😖

Add a description _____

_____

_____

READ:

Proverbs 3:5-6

"Trust in the Lord with all your heart and lean not on your own understanding; In all your ways acknowledge Him, and He shall direct your paths."

REFLECT:

Identify areas where you need to trust God more

_____

_____

_____

_____

_____

_____

ACTION:

Write a prayer asking God to help you trust Him in those areas. Trusting God can be challenging, especially in uncertain times. By pinpointing specific areas and praying about them, you invite God's guidance and reassurance into your life.

_____

_____

_____

_____

_____

_____

BRENDAJEFFERSON.COM

30 DAY JOURNEY TO BOLD FAITH

Week 1 " Laying the Foundation of Bold Faith"   Date ____ / ____ / ____

Day 4: Pray with Faith

How do you feel today?

Choose a face 😁 😊 😐 😟 😢 😠

Add a description _____

_____

_____

READ:

Mark 11:24

"Therefore I say to you, whatever things you ask when you pray, believe that you receive them, and you will have them."

REFLECT:

Think about something you need to pray for with. Then, act on it.

ACTION:

Pray boldly for something specific, believing that God will answer. This verse teaches the importance of praying with belief. By choosing something specific to pray for, you practice putting this verse into action, reinforcing your faith in God's power and willingness to respond.

_____

_____

_____

_____

_____

BRENDAJEFFERSON.COM

30 DAY JOURNEY TO BOLD FAITH

Week 1 " Laying the Foundation of Bold Faith"   Date ____ / ____ / ____
Day 5: Meditate on God's Word

How do you feel today?

Choose a face 😁 🙂 😐 🙁 😣 😫

Add a description _____

_____

_____

READ:

Joshua 1:8

"This Book of the Law shall not depart from your mouth, but you shall meditate in it day and night, that you may observe to do according to all that is written in it. For then you will make your way prosperous, and then you will have good success."

REFLECT:

Consider the benefits of meditating on God's Word daily.

ACTION:

Set aside time each day to read and meditate on a passage of Scripture. Meditating on God's Word helps you internalize His promises and commands, fostering a deeper understanding and a stronger faith.

_____

_____

_____

_____

_____

_____

30 DAY JOURNEY TO BOLD FAITH

Week 1 " Laying the Foundation of Bold Faith" Date ___ / ___ / ___
Day 6: Build Your Confidence in God

How do you feel today?

Choose a face 😁 😊 😐 🙁 🥺 😣

Add a description _____

_____

_____

READ:

Philippians 4:13

"I can do all things through Christ who strengthens me."

REFLECT:

Reflect on a situation where you need God's strength. How can you invite Him into your situation?

_____

_____

_____

ACTION:

Write down a personal affirmation based on this verse to remind yourself of God's power in your life. This verse instills confidence by reminding you that God's strength is available to you. Creating a personal affirmation reinforces this truth and helps you approach challenges with a bold mindset.

_____

_____

_____

_____

_____

BRENDAJEFFERSON.COM

30 DAY JOURNEY TO BOLD FAITH

Week 1 " Laying the Foundation of Bold Faith"   Date ____ / ____ / ____
Day 7: Praise God in All Circumstances

How do you feel today?

Choose a face

Add a description _____

_____

_____

> **READ:**
>
> **1 Thessalonians 5:18**
>
> "In everything give thanks; for this is the will of God in Christ Jesus for you."

REFLECT:

Think about how you can thank God even in difficult situations.

_____

_____

_____

_____

_____

_____

ACTION:

Start a gratitude journal, noting at least one thing you are thankful for each day. Praising God in all circumstances helps shift your focus from problems to His blessings, fostering a positive and faith-filled outlook.

_____

_____

_____

_____

_____

_____

BRENDAJEFFERSON.COM

30 DAY JOURNEY TO BOLD FAITH

Week 2 "Growing in Bold Faith"
Day 8: Believe in God's Promises

Date ____ / ____ / ____

How do you feel today?

Choose a face 😄 😊 😐 🙁 🥺 😣

Add a description _____

_____

_____

READ:

2 Corinthians 1:20

"For all the promises of God in Him are Yes, and in Him Amen, to the glory of God through us."

REFLECT:

Identify a promise of God that you need to believe in today.

ACTION:

Write down the promise and place it somewhere visible as a daily reminder. This practice keeps God's promises at the forefront of your mind, reinforcing your faith in His reliability.

BRENDAJEFFERSON.COM

30 DAY JOURNEY TO BOLD FAITH

Week 2 "Growing in Bold Faith"
Day 9: Live by Faith, Not by Sight

Date ____ / ____ / ____

How do you feel today?

Choose a face

Add a description _____

_____

_____

READ:

2 Corinthians 5:7

"For we walk by faith, not by sight."

REFLECT:

Consider an area of your life where you are relying too much on what you see rather than on faith.

ACTION:

Take a step of faith in that area, trusting God beyond 2551 your current circumstances. This helps you practice living by faith, fostering trust in God's unseen plans.

30 DAY JOURNEY TO BOLD FAITH

Week 2 "Growing in Bold Faith"
Day 10: Embrace God's Peace

Date ____ / ____ / ____

How do you feel today?

Choose a face

Add a description _____

_____

_____

READ:

Philippians 4:6-7

"Be anxious for nothing, but in everything by prayer and supplication, with thanksgiving, let your requests be made known to God; and the peace of God, which surpasses all understanding, will guard your hearts and minds through Christ Jesus."

REFLECT:

Identify a worry that you need to surrender to God.

_____

_____

_____

_____

_____

ACTION:

Pray about it and thank God for His peace, trusting 2561 Him to handle your concerns. This encourages you to exchange anxiety for peace through prayer, deepening your reliance on God.

_____

_____

_____

_____

_____

_____

BRENDAJEFFERSON.COM

30 DAY JOURNEY TO BOLD FAITH

Week 2 "Growing in Bold Faith"
Day 11: Act on Your Faith

Date ____ / ____ / ____

How do you feel today?

Choose a face

Add a description _____

_____

_____

READ:

James 2:17

"Thus also faith by itself, if it does not have works, is dead."

REFLECT:

Think about a practical way you can demonstrate your faith today.

ACTION:

Perform an act of kindness or service as an expression of your faith. This reinforces that true faith is active and impactful.

brendajefferson.com

30 DAY JOURNEY TO BOLD FAITH

Week 2 "Growing in Bold Faith"
Day 12: Stand Firm in Faith

Date ____ / ____ / ____

How do you feel today?

Choose a face 😁 😊 😐 🙁 🥺 😠

Add a description _____

_____

_____

READ:

Ephesians 6:16

"Above all, taking the shield of faith with which you will be able to quench all the fiery darts of the wicked one."

REFLECT:

Consider the challenges that test your faith.

ACTION:

Pray for strength to stand firm and identify a scripture that strengthens your resolve. This equips you to face spiritual battles with God's Word as your defense.

_____

_____

_____

_____

_____

BRENDAJEFFERSON.COM

30 DAY JOURNEY TO BOLD FAITH

Week 2 "Growing in Bold Faith"
Day 13: Speak Words of Faith

Date ____ / ____ / ____

How do you feel today?

Choose a face

Add a description _____

_____

_____

READ:

Proverbs 18:21

"Death and life are in the power of the tongue, and those who love it will eat its fruit."

REFLECT:

Reflect on the power of your words.

ACTION:

Make a conscious effort to speak positive and faith filled words throughout the day. This cultivates an atmosphere of faith and positivity around you.

30 DAY JOURNEY TO BOLD FAITH

Week 2 "Growing in Bold Faith"
Day 14: Reflect on God's Faithfulness

Date ____ / ____ / ____

How do you feel today?

Choose a face

Add a description _____

_____

_____

READ:

Lamentations 3:22-23

"Through the Lord's mercies we are not consumed, because His compassions fail not. They are new every morning; Great is Your faithfulness."

REFLECT:

Remember times when God has been faithful to you.

_____
_____
_____
_____
_____

ACTION:

Write a thank-you note to God for His faithfulness in your life. Reflecting on God's past faithfulness builds your faith for the future.

_____
_____
_____
_____
_____
_____
_____

30 DAY JOURNEY TO BOLD FAITH

Week 3 " Deepening Your Bold Faith"   Date ____ / ____ / ____
Day 15: Surrender Completely to God

How do you feel today?

Choose a face

Add a description _____

_____

_____

READ:

Romans 12:1

"I beseech you therefore, brethren, by the mercies of God, that you present your bodies a living sacrifice, holy, acceptable to God, which is your reasonable service."

REFLECT:

Identify areas you need to surrender to God.

ACTION:

Commit these areas to God in prayer, asking for His help to fully surrender. Surrendering to God brings freedom and aligns your life with His will.

30 DAY JOURNEY TO BOLD FAITH

Week 3 " Deepening Your Bold Faith"
Day 16: Keep Your Focus on Jesus

Date ____ / ____ / ____

How do you feel today?

Choose a face

Add a description _____

_____

_____

READ:

Hebrews 12:2

"Looking unto Jesus, the author and finisher of our faith, who for the joy that was set before Him endured the cross, despising the shame, and has sat down at the right hand of the throne of God."

REFLECT:

Consider distractions that take your focus off Jesus.

ACTION:

Eliminate one distraction today and spend that time focusing on Jesus. Maintaining focus on Jesus strengthens your faith and helps you navigate life's challenges.

BRENDAJEFFERSON.COM

30 DAY JOURNEY TO BOLD FAITH

Week 3 " Deepening Your Bold Faith"
Day 17: Be Persistent in Prayer

Date ____ / ____ / ____

How do you feel today?

Choose a face

Add a description _____

_____

_____

READ:

Luke 18:1

"Then He spoke a parable to them, that men always ought to pray and not lose heart."

REFLECT:

Reflect on the importance of persistence in prayer.

ACTION:

Choose a prayer request to persistently bring before God each day this week. Persistence in prayer deepens your relationship with God and demonstrates unwavering faith

30 DAY JOURNEY TO BOLD FAITH

Week 3 " Deepening Your Bold Faith"
Day 18: Trust God's Timing

Date ____ / ____ / ____

How do you feel today?

Choose a face 😄 😊 😐 ☹️ 🥺 😠

Add a description _____

_____

_____

READ:

Ecclesiastes 3:11

"He has made everything beautiful in its time. Also, He has put eternity in their hearts, except that no one can find out the work that God does from beginning to end."

REFLECT:

Think about a situation where you need to trust God's timing.

_____

_____

_____

_____

ACTION:

Pray for patience and trust in God's perfect timing. Trusting God's timing brings peace and patience, knowing His plans are perfect.

_____

_____

_____

_____

_____

_____

30 DAY JOURNEY TO BOLD FAITH

Week 3 " Deepening Your Bold Faith"
Day 19: Rejoice in the Lord

Date ____ / ____ / ____

How do you feel today?

Choose a face

Add a description _____

_____

_____

READ:

Philippians 4:4

"Rejoice in the Lord always. Again, I will say, rejoice!"

REFLECT:

Identify reasons to rejoice in the Lord today.

ACTION:

Spend time praising and rejoicing in God's goodness. Rejoicing in the Lord lifts your spirit and strengthens your faith.

BRENDAJEFFERSON.COM

30 DAY JOURNEY TO BOLD FAITH

Week 3 " Deepening Your Bold Faith"
Day 20: Be Still and Know God

Date ____ / ____ / ____

How do you feel today?

Choose a face

Add a description _____

_____

_____

READ:

Psalm 46:10

"Be still and know that I am God; I will be exalted among the nations, I will be exalted in the earth!"

REFLECT:

Contemplate the importance of being still before God. How can you make time to be in His presence?

ACTION:

Set aside time to be still and reflect on God's presence in your life. Being still before God allows you to hear His voice and strengthens your faith.

30 DAY JOURNEY TO BOLD FAITH

Week 3 "Deepening Your Bold Faith" Date ____ / ____ / ____
Day 21: Share Your Faith

How do you feel today?

Choose a face

Add a description _____

_____

READ:

Matthew 5:16

"Let your light so shine before men, that they may see your good works and glorify your Father in Heaven."

REFLECT:

Think about how your faith can be a light to others.

ACTION:

Share a testimony or encouraging word with someone today. Sharing your faith reinforces it within you and spreads hope to others.

BRENDAJEFFERSON.COM

30 DAY JOURNEY TO BOLD FAITH

Week 4 " Strengthening and Sustaining Bold Faith" Date ____ / ____ / ____
Day 22: Remember God's Promises

How do you feel today?

Choose a face

Add a description _____

_____

_____

READ:

2 Peter 1:4

"By which have been given to us exceedingly great and precious promises, that through these you may be partakers of the divine nature, having escaped the corruption that is in the world through lust."

REFLECT:

Recall a promise of God that has impacted you.

_____
_____
_____
_____
_____
_____

ACTION:

Write it down and reflect on how it applies to your current situation. Remembering God's promises strengthens your faith and provides encouragement.

_____
_____
_____
_____
_____
_____
_____

30 DAY JOURNEY TO BOLD FAITH

Week 4 " Strengthening and Sustaining Bold Faith"   Date ____ / ____ / ____

Day 23: Walk in the Spirit

How do you feel today?

Choose a face

Add a description _____

_____

_____

READ:

Galatians 5:16

"I say then: Walk in the Spirit, and you shall not fulfill the lust of the flesh."

REFLECT:

Consider how you can be more attuned to the Holy Spirit's guidance.

ACTION:

Pray for the Holy Spirit to guide your actions and decisions today. Walking in the Spirit aligns your life with God's will and strengthens your faith.

30 DAY JOURNEY TO BOLD FAITH

Week 4 " Strengthening and Sustaining Bold Faith" Date ____ / ____ / ____
Day 24: Overcome Fear with Faith

How do you feel today?

Choose a face 😄 😊 😐 🙁 😢 😣

Add a description _____

_____

_____

READ:

Isaiah 41:10

"Fear not, for I am with you; Be not dismayed, for I am your God. I will strengthen you, yes, I will help you, I will uphold you with My righteous right hand."

REFLECT:

Identify a fear you need to overcome with faith.

ACTION:

Confront that fear, trusting in God's presence and help. Overcoming fear with faith builds confidence in God's power and care.

BRENDAJEFFERSON.COM

30 DAY JOURNEY TO BOLD FAITH

Week 4 " Strengthening and Sustaining Bold Faith"   Date ____ / ____ / ____

Day 25: Be Generous

How do you feel today?

Choose a face

Add a description _____

_____

_____

READ:

2 Corinthians 9:6-7

"But this I say: He who sows sparingly will also reap sparingly, and he who sows bountifully will also reap bountifully. So let each one give as he purposes in his heart, not grudgingly or of necessity; for God loves a cheerful giver."

REFLECT:

Reflect on the blessings of generosity.

ACTION:

Give generously to someone in need, trusting God to bless your giving. Generosity reflects God's heart and strengthens your faith in His provision.

30 DAY JOURNEY TO BOLD FAITH

Week 4 " Strengthening and Sustaining Bold Faith"   Date ____ / ____ / ____
Day 26: Embrace God's Grace

How do you feel today?

Choose a face

Add a description _____

_____

_____

READ:

2 Corinthians 12:9

"And He said to me, 'My grace is sufficient for you, for My strength is made perfect in weakness.' Therefore, most gladly I will rather boast in my infirmities, that the power of Christ may rest upon me."

REFLECT:

Think about areas where you need God's grace.

ACTION:

Pray for His grace to empower you in your weaknesses. Embracing God's grace strengthens your reliance on His power.

30 DAY JOURNEY TO BOLD FAITH

Week 4 " Strengthening and Sustaining Bold Faith"   Date ____ / ____ / ____

Day 27: Keep Your Heart Pure

How do you feel today?

Choose a face

Add a description _____

_____

_____

READ:

Psalm 51:10

"Create in me a clean heart, O God, and renew a steadfast spirit within me."

REFLECT:

Identify any attitudes or habits that need cleansing.

ACTION:

Ask God to purify your heart and renew your spirit. A pure heart is essential for strong and bold faith.

BRENDAJEFFERSON.COM

30 DAY JOURNEY TO BOLD FAITH

Week 4 " Strengthening and Sustaining Bold Faith" Date ___ / ___ / ___
Day 28: Be Courageous

How do you feel today?

Choose a face

Add a description _____

_____

_____

READ:

Joshua 1:9
"Have I not commanded you? Be strong and of good courage; do not be afraid, nor be dismayed, for the Lord your God is with you wherever you go."

REFLECT:
Consider an area where you need to show courage.

ACTION:

Take a step of courage, knowing God is with you. Courage in action strengthens your faith and reliance on God.

_____

_____

_____

_____

_____

_____

_____

BRENDAJEFFERSON.COM

30 DAY JOURNEY TO BOLD FAITH

Week 4 " Strengthening and Sustaining Bold Faith"   Date ____ / ____ / ____

Day 29: Reflect God's Love

How do you feel today?

Choose a face

Add a description _____

_____

_____

READ:

John 13:34-35

"A new commandment I give to you, that you love one another; as I have loved you, that you also love one another. By this all will know that you are My disciples, if you have love for one another."

REFLECT:

Think about how you can show God's love to others.

ACTION:

Perform an act of love for someone today. Reflecting God's love demonstrates your faith and strengthens your connection to others.

BRENDAJEFFERSON.COM

30 DAY JOURNEY TO BOLD FAITH

Week 4 " Strengthening and Sustaining Bold Faith"   Date ____ / ____ / ____
Day 30: Stay Committed to Faith

How do you feel today?

Choose a face 😃 ☺️ 😐 🙁 😣 😖

Add a description _____
_____
_____

READ:

Hebrews 10:23

"Let us hold fast the confession of our hope without wavering, for He who promised is faithful."

REFLECT:

Consider how you can maintain your commitment to bold faith.

ACTION:

: Make a personal commitment to continue growing in faith. Staying committed to faith ensures continuous growth and deepens your relationship with God.

BRENDAJEFFERSON.COM

CLOSING REFLECTION AND PRAYER

REFLECTION:

As you come to the end of this 30-Day Journey to Bold Faith, take a moment to reflect on the transformation that has taken place within you. You have laid the foundation of faith, deepened your trust in God, and discovered new ways to live boldly for His purpose. Through scripture, reflection, and action, you have experienced growth—both in your relationship with God and in your understanding of what it means to walk by faith.

This journey was not just about completing a series of daily exercises but about cultivating a deeper connection with God. You have strengthened your spiritual muscles, learned to rely on God in new ways, and embraced the call to live a life set apart. Each step you've taken has brought you closer to Him, and this is only the beginning.

The transformation that has begun in these 30 days will continue as you carry forward the lessons, practices, and bold faith you have embraced. Let this be a foundation upon which you build a life of purpose, trust, and unwavering faith in God. Remember, living boldly in faith is a daily decision, a journey of continual growth, and a testament to the power of God working through you.

As you step forward from this moment, trust that God is with you in every step, guiding, strengthening, and empowering you to live out His calling on your life. Continue to seek Him first, trust Him fully, and watch as He unfolds His plans for you in ways you never imagined.

PRAYER:

Heavenly Father,

Thank You for guiding me through this journey of bold faith. I am grateful for the transformation that has taken place in my heart and the new depths of trust I have discovered in You. Lord, You have opened my eyes to Your truth and filled me with the courage to live out my faith boldly. I ask that You continue to strengthen my spirit and remind me daily of Your promises.

As I move forward, help me to carry the lessons I've learned, to keep seeking You first in all things, and to trust in Your perfect plan for my life. May my faith continue to grow, may my heart stay open to Your guidance, and may my actions reflect Your love and glory. Lead me in every decision, and give me the boldness to walk in the purpose You have set before me.

Thank You for Your unending grace, Your faithfulness, and the way You continue to shape and refine me. I trust You with my future, knowing that You will guide me every step of the way.

In Jesus' name,
Amen.

NOTES

NOTES

NOTES

NOTES

BRENDA JEFFERSON
AUTHOR

Dr Brenda Jefferson is essential to the body of Christ. Her passion for the Word of God, gospel music, worship, and her creative ability to write, allows her to inspire others in a positive way. She is a bright light in the lives of many, embarking for change and calling others toward Holiness.

Through the mission and ministry of her husband, Bishop M.B. Jefferson, she is Co-Pastor of Living in Victory Christian Church, Deep Life Christian Church, and World Assemblies Fellowship International. She also helps to oversee The House of David Help Center and is CEO of Scripture Music Group.

With ministry at the forefront of her heart, she is submissive to the call of God on her life. Together, they work diligently to release strongholds, unite relationships, deliver those bound from addiction, empower the youth, and be a united influence for Jesus. In these uncertain times of pandemic, poverty, wars, and famine, she is necessary for this generation. Her 'last days' message of repentance, faith, and good works captivates the masses. Through truth and humility, she is devoted to her assignment and seeks to help those in need.

OTHER WORKS BY DR. BRENDA JEFFERSON

BOOKS

Seasons

Praise Him While You Wait

Rhema Through My Song

Triumph Through Pain

MUSIC & ALBUMS

Lamb of God

A Time of Refreshing

Triumph Through Pain

Supernatural

Invocation

Miracle

Stay Connected and Follow Us:

YouTube Channel: Dr. Brenda Jefferson

Instagram: DrBrendaJ

www.brendajefferson.com

www.livcc.org

www.ingramcontent.com/pod-product-compliance
Lightning Source LLC
Chambersburg PA
CBHW072208070526
44585CB00015B/1246